C000015880

Data Preparation Tools
Complete Self-Assessment Guide

The guidance in this Self-Assessment is based on Data Preparation Tools best practices and standards in business process architecture, design and quality management. The guidance is also based on the professional judgment of the individual collaborators listed in the Acknowledgments.

Notice of rights

You are licensed to use the Self-Assessment contents in your presentations and materials for internal use and customers without asking us - we are here to help.

Trademarks

Table of Contents

About The Art of Service

The Art of Service, Business Process Architects since 2000, is dedicated to helping stakeholders achieve excellence.

Defining, designing, creating, and implementing a process to solve a stakeholders challenge or meet an objective is the most valuable role... In EVERY group, company, organization and department.

Unless you're talking a one-time, single-use project, there should be a process. Whether that process is managed and implemented by humans, AI, or a combination of the two, it needs to be designed by someone with a complex enough perspective to ask the right questions.

Someone capable of asking the right questions and step back and say, 'What are we really trying to accomplish here? And is there a different way to look at it?'

With The Art of Service's Standard Requirements Self-Assessments, we empower people who can do just that — whether their title is marketer, entrepreneur, manager, salesperson, consultant, Business Process Manager, executive assistant, IT Manager, CIO etc... —they are the people who rule the future. They are people who watch the process as it happens, and ask the right questions to make the process work better.

Contact us when you need any support with this Self-Assessment and any help with templates, blue-prints and examples of standard documents you might need:

http://theartofservice.com
service@theartofservice.com

Included Resources - how to access

Included with your purchase of the book is the Data Preparation

Tools Self-Assessment Spreadsheet Dashboard which contains all questions and Self-Assessment areas and auto-generates insights, graphs, and project RACI planning - all with examples to get you started right away.

How? Simply send an email to
access@theartofservice.com
with this books' title in the subject to get the Data Preparation Tools Self Assessment Tool right away.

You will receive the following contents with New and Updated specific criteria:

- The latest quick edition of the book in PDF

- The latest complete edition of the book in PDF, which criteria correspond to the criteria in...

- The Self-Assessment Excel Dashboard, and...

- Example pre-filled Self-Assessment Excel Dashboard to get familiar with results generation

- In-depth specific Checklists covering the topic

- Project management checklists and templates to assist with implementation

INCLUDES LIFETIME SELF ASSESSMENT UPDATES

Every self assessment comes with Lifetime Updates and Lifetime Free Updated Books. Lifetime Updates is an industry-first feature which allows you to receive verified self assessment updates, ensuring you always have the most accurate information at your fingertips.

Get it now- you will be glad you did - do it now, before you forget.

Send an email to **access@theartofservice.com** with this books' title in the subject to get the Data Preparation Tools Self Assessment Tool right away.

Purpose of this Self-Assessment

This Self-Assessment has been developed to improve understanding of the requirements and elements of Data Preparation Tools, based on best practices and standards in business process architecture, design and quality management.

It is designed to allow for a rapid Self-Assessment to determine how closely existing management practices and procedures correspond to the elements of the Self-Assessment.

The criteria of requirements and elements of Data Preparation Tools have been rephrased in the format of a Self-Assessment questionnaire, with a seven-criterion scoring system, as explained in this document.

In this format, even with limited background knowledge of Data Preparation Tools, a manager can quickly review existing operations to determine how they measure up to the standards. This in turn can serve as the starting point of a 'gap analysis' to identify management tools or system elements that might usefully be implemented in the organization to help improve overall performance.

How to use the Self-Assessment

On the following pages are a series of questions to identify to what extent your Data Preparation Tools initiative is complete in comparison to the requirements set in standards.

To facilitate answering the questions, there is a space in front of each question to enter a score on a scale of '1' to '5'.

1 Strongly Disagree

2 Disagree

3 Neutral

4 Agree

5 Strongly Agree

Read the question and rate it with the following in front of mind:

'In my belief, the answer to this question is clearly defined'.

There are two ways in which you can choose to interpret this statement;
1. how aware are you that the answer to the question is clearly defined
2. for more in-depth analysis you can choose to gather evidence and confirm the answer to the question. This obviously will take more time, most Self-Assessment users opt for the first way to interpret the question and dig deeper later on based on the outcome of the overall Self-Assessment.

A score of '1' would mean that the answer is not clear at all, where a '5' would mean the answer is crystal clear and defined. Leave emtpy when the question is not applicable or you don't want to answer it, you can skip it without affecting your score. Write your score in the space provided.

After you have responded to all the appropriate statements in each section, compute your average score for that section, using the formula provided, and round to the nearest tenth. Then transfer to the corresponding spoke in the Data Preparation Tools Scorecard on the second next page of the Self-Assessment.

Your completed Data Preparation Tools Scorecard will give you a clear presentation of which Data Preparation Tools areas need attention.

Data Preparation Tools
Scorecard Example

Example of how the finalized Scorecard can look like:

Data Preparation Tools Scorecard

Your Scores:

BEGINNING OF THE SELF-ASSESSMENT:

CRITERION #1: RECOGNIZE

INTENT: Be aware of the need for change. Recognize that there is an unfavorable variation, problem or symptom.

In my belief, the answer to this question is clearly defined:

5 Strongly Agree

4 Agree

3 Neutral

2 Disagree

1 Strongly Disagree

1. What are the timeframes required to resolve each of the issues/problems?
<--- Score

2. Does your organization need more Data Preparation Tools education?
<--- Score

3. Who else hopes to benefit from it?

<--- Score

4. What training and capacity building actions are needed to implement proposed reforms?
<--- Score

5. How do you assess your Data Preparation Tools workforce capability and capacity needs, including skills, competencies, and staffing levels?
<--- Score

6. What is the extent or complexity of the Data Preparation Tools problem?
<--- Score

7. What do employees need in the short term?
<--- Score

8. Think about the people you identified for your Data Preparation Tools project and the project responsibilities you would assign to them, what kind of training do you think they would need to perform these responsibilities effectively?
<--- Score

9. Will a response program recognize when a crisis occurs and provide some level of response?
<--- Score

10. Will Data Preparation Tools deliverables need to be tested and, if so, by whom?
<--- Score

11. Would you recognize a threat from the inside?
<--- Score

12. What resources or support might you need?
<--- Score

13. Do you recognize Data Preparation Tools achievements?
<--- Score

14. Did you miss any major Data Preparation Tools issues?
<--- Score

15. What are the Data Preparation Tools resources needed?
<--- Score

16. Why the need?
<--- Score

17. How do you identify the kinds of information that you will need?
<--- Score

18. How are you going to measure success?
<--- Score

19. Are problem definition and motivation clearly presented?
<--- Score

20. For your Data Preparation Tools project, identify and describe the business environment, is there more than one layer to the business environment?
<--- Score

21. What tools and technologies are needed for a custom Data Preparation Tools project?

<--- Score

22. What is the smallest subset of the problem you can usefully solve?
<--- Score

23. How much are sponsors, customers, partners, stakeholders involved in Data Preparation Tools? In other words, what are the risks, if Data Preparation Tools does not deliver successfully?
<--- Score

24. What are the stakeholder objectives to be achieved with Data Preparation Tools?
<--- Score

25. How do you recognize an Data Preparation Tools objection?
<--- Score

26. Are your goals realistic? Do you need to redefine your problem? Perhaps the problem has changed or maybe you have reached your goal and need to set a new one?
<--- Score

27. What extra resources will you need?
<--- Score

28. Why is this needed?
<--- Score

29. Is it needed?
<--- Score

30. Does the problem have ethical dimensions?

<--- Score

31. Looking at each person individually – does every one have the qualities which are needed to work in this group?
<--- Score

32. What Data Preparation Tools events should you attend?
<--- Score

33. What is the Data Preparation Tools problem definition? What do you need to resolve?
<--- Score

34. Do you have/need 24-hour access to key personnel?
<--- Score

35. Who defines the rules in relation to any given issue?
<--- Score

36. What creative shifts do you need to take?
<--- Score

37. Are employees recognized or rewarded for performance that demonstrates the highest levels of integrity?
<--- Score

38. Do you know what you need to know about Data Preparation Tools?
<--- Score

39. Who needs budgets?

<--- Score

40. What are the expected benefits of Data Preparation Tools to the stakeholder?
<--- Score

41. What is the recognized need?
<--- Score

42. What is the problem and/or vulnerability?
<--- Score

43. Which issues are too important to ignore?
<--- Score

44. What are the minority interests and what amount of minority interests can be recognized?
<--- Score

45. What Data Preparation Tools coordination do you need?
<--- Score

46. Whom do you really need or want to serve?
<--- Score

47. How does it fit into your organizational needs and tasks?
<--- Score

48. Are there any revenue recognition issues?
<--- Score

49. As a sponsor, customer or management, how important is it to meet goals, objectives?
<--- Score

50. Are controls defined to recognize and contain problems?

<--- Score

51. Will it solve real problems?

<--- Score

52. Have you identified your Data Preparation Tools key performance indicators?

<--- Score

53. How are training requirements identified?

<--- Score

54. Who needs what information?

<--- Score

55. What Data Preparation Tools capabilities do you need?

<--- Score

56. How do you recognize an objection?

<--- Score

57. Are there recognized Data Preparation Tools problems?

<--- Score

58. What else needs to be measured?

<--- Score

59. What should be considered when identifying available resources, constraints, and deadlines?

<--- Score

60. Who needs to know about Data Preparation Tools?

<--- Score

61. When a Data Preparation Tools manager recognizes a problem, what options are available?

<--- Score

62. Who should resolve the Data Preparation Tools issues?

<--- Score

63. What vendors make products that address the Data Preparation Tools needs?

<--- Score

64. What needs to stay?

<--- Score

65. What are the clients issues and concerns?

<--- Score

66. How can auditing be a preventative security measure?

<--- Score

67. What would happen if Data Preparation Tools weren't done?

<--- Score

68. What prevents you from making the changes you know will make you a more effective Data Preparation Tools leader?

<--- Score

69. Is it clear when you think of the day ahead of you

what activities and tasks you need to complete?
<--- Score

70. Is the quality assurance team identified?
<--- Score

71. Does Data Preparation Tools create potential expectations in other areas that need to be recognized and considered?
<--- Score

72. What Data Preparation Tools problem should be solved?
<--- Score

73. Who needs to know?
<--- Score

74. Are there any specific expectations or concerns about the Data Preparation Tools team, Data Preparation Tools itself?
<--- Score

75. How do you take a forward-looking perspective in identifying Data Preparation Tools research related to market response and models?
<--- Score

76. Do you need different information or graphics?
<--- Score

77. What activities does the governance board need to consider?
<--- Score

78. How many trainings, in total, are needed?

<--- Score

79. Which needs are not included or involved?
<--- Score

80. What does Data Preparation Tools success mean to the stakeholders?
<--- Score

81. Will new equipment/products be required to facilitate Data Preparation Tools delivery, for example is new software needed?
<--- Score

82. To what extent does each concerned units management team recognize Data Preparation Tools as an effective investment?
<--- Score

83. How are the Data Preparation Tools's objectives aligned to the group's overall stakeholder strategy?
<--- Score

84. What situation(s) led to this Data Preparation Tools Self Assessment?
<--- Score

85. Where do you need to exercise leadership?
<--- Score

86. What do you need to start doing?
<--- Score

87. What problems are you facing and how do you consider Data Preparation Tools will circumvent those obstacles?

<--- Score

88. Who are your key stakeholders who need to sign off?
<--- Score

89. Are there regulatory / compliance issues?
<--- Score

90. Can management personnel recognize the monetary benefit of Data Preparation Tools?
<--- Score

91. What information do users need?
<--- Score

92. Are employees recognized for desired behaviors?
<--- Score

93. Do you need to avoid or amend any Data Preparation Tools activities?
<--- Score

94. What needs to be done?
<--- Score

95. Where is training needed?
<--- Score

96. What is the problem or issue?
<--- Score

97. Are there Data Preparation Tools problems defined?
<--- Score

98. To what extent would your organization benefit from being recognized as a award recipient?
<--- Score

Add up total points for this section:
_ _ _ _ _ = Total points for this section

Divided by: _ _ _ _ _ _ (number of statements answered) = _ _ _ _ _ _
Average score for this section

Transfer your score to the Data Preparation Tools Index at the beginning of the Self-Assessment.

CRITERION #2: DEFINE:

INTENT: Formulate the stakeholder problem. Define the problem, needs and objectives.

In my belief, the answer to this question is clearly defined:

5 Strongly Agree

4 Agree

3 Neutral

2 Disagree

1 Strongly Disagree

1. Why are you doing Data Preparation Tools and what is the scope?
<--- Score

2. Is the Data Preparation Tools scope manageable?
<--- Score

3. What are the core elements of the Data Preparation Tools business case?

<--- Score

4. How do you gather the stories?
<--- Score

5. How would you define Data Preparation Tools leadership?
<--- Score

6. Who approved the Data Preparation Tools scope?
<--- Score

7. How and when will the baselines be defined?
<--- Score

8. What knowledge or experience is required?
<--- Score

9. Have all basic functions of Data Preparation Tools been defined?
<--- Score

10. What system do you use for gathering Data Preparation Tools information?
<--- Score

11. How do you think the partners involved in Data Preparation Tools would have defined success?
<--- Score

12. Is there regularly 100% attendance at the team meetings? If not, have appointed substitutes attended to preserve cross-functionality and full representation?
<--- Score

13. When is the estimated completion date?
<--- Score

14. How is the team tracking and documenting its work?
<--- Score

15. How will the Data Preparation Tools team and the group measure complete success of Data Preparation Tools?
<--- Score

16. Has a team charter been developed and communicated?
<--- Score

17. How will variation in the actual durations of each activity be dealt with to ensure that the expected Data Preparation Tools results are met?
<--- Score

18. Is the team equipped with available and reliable resources?
<--- Score

19. Is there a critical path to deliver Data Preparation Tools results?
<--- Score

20. What are the Data Preparation Tools use cases?
<--- Score

21. What are the requirements for audit information?
<--- Score

22. Has anyone else (internal or external to the group)

attempted to solve this problem or a similar one before? If so, what knowledge can be leveraged from these previous efforts?

<--- Score

23. What customer feedback methods were used to solicit their input?

<--- Score

24. How does the Data Preparation Tools manager ensure against scope creep?

<--- Score

25. Are the Data Preparation Tools requirements complete?

<--- Score

26. How do you catch Data Preparation Tools definition inconsistencies?

<--- Score

27. The political context: who holds power?

<--- Score

28. How do you hand over Data Preparation Tools context?

<--- Score

29. Is there a completed SIPOC representation, describing the Suppliers, Inputs, Process, Outputs, and Customers?

<--- Score

30. How was the 'as is' process map developed, reviewed, verified and validated?

<--- Score

31. Are audit criteria, scope, frequency and methods defined?
<--- Score

32. What sort of initial information to gather?
<--- Score

33. Will team members perform Data Preparation Tools work when assigned and in a timely fashion?
<--- Score

34. What happens if Data Preparation Tools's scope changes?
<--- Score

35. How would you define the culture at your organization, how susceptible is it to Data Preparation Tools changes?
<--- Score

36. Have the customer needs been translated into specific, measurable requirements? How?
<--- Score

37. What Data Preparation Tools services do you require?
<--- Score

38. Is Data Preparation Tools required?
<--- Score

39. What is the context?
<--- Score

40. What is out of scope?

<--- Score

41. What scope to assess?
<--- Score

42. Is there a Data Preparation Tools management charter, including stakeholder case, problem and goal statements, scope, milestones, roles and responsibilities, communication plan?
<--- Score

43. Is the team adequately staffed with the desired cross-functionality? If not, what additional resources are available to the team?
<--- Score

44. Has the Data Preparation Tools work been fairly and/or equitably divided and delegated among team members who are qualified and capable to perform the work? Has everyone contributed?
<--- Score

45. In what way can you redefine the criteria of choice clients have in your category in your favor?
<--- Score

46. How do you manage changes in Data Preparation Tools requirements?
<--- Score

47. What are the boundaries of the scope? What is in bounds and what is not? What is the start point? What is the stop point?
<--- Score

48. Has a high-level 'as is' process map been

completed, verified and validated?
<--- Score

49. What was the context?
<--- Score

50. What is the definition of Data Preparation Tools excellence?
<--- Score

51. What are the Roles and Responsibilities for each team member and its leadership? Where is this documented?
<--- Score

52. Have specific policy objectives been defined?
<--- Score

53. Is data collected and displayed to better understand customer(s) critical needs and requirements.
<--- Score

54. Is there a completed, verified, and validated high-level 'as is' (not 'should be' or 'could be') stakeholder process map?
<--- Score

55. Are all requirements met?
<--- Score

56. Is there any additional Data Preparation Tools definition of success?
<--- Score

57. Is Data Preparation Tools linked to key stakeholder

goals and objectives?

<--- Score

58. Does the scope remain the same?

<--- Score

59. Will team members regularly document their Data Preparation Tools work?

<--- Score

60. Has the direction changed at all during the course of Data Preparation Tools? If so, when did it change and why?

<--- Score

61. How do you manage scope?

<--- Score

62. What is the scope of Data Preparation Tools?

<--- Score

63. How do you gather requirements?

<--- Score

64. What key stakeholder process output measure(s) does Data Preparation Tools leverage and how?

<--- Score

65. What baselines are required to be defined and managed?

<--- Score

66. Who defines (or who defined) the rules and roles?

<--- Score

67. How do you build the right business case?

<--- Score

68. What gets examined?
<--- Score

69. How often are the team meetings?
<--- Score

70. What information do you gather?
<--- Score

71. Are the Data Preparation Tools requirements testable?
<--- Score

72. What are the compelling stakeholder reasons for embarking on Data Preparation Tools?
<--- Score

73. Will a Data Preparation Tools production readiness review be required?
<--- Score

74. What is in the scope and what is not in scope?
<--- Score

75. Has everyone on the team, including the team leaders, been properly trained?
<--- Score

76. Scope of sensitive information?
<--- Score

77. What intelligence can you gather?
<--- Score

78. How do you manage unclear Data Preparation Tools requirements?

<--- Score

79. How do you keep key subject matter experts in the loop?

<--- Score

80. Is the Data Preparation Tools scope complete and appropriately sized?

<--- Score

81. Where can you gather more information?

<--- Score

82. What sources do you use to gather information for a Data Preparation Tools study?

<--- Score

83. Have all of the relationships been defined properly?

<--- Score

84. Are there different segments of customers?

<--- Score

85. If substitutes have been appointed, have they been briefed on the Data Preparation Tools goals and received regular communications as to the progress to date?

<--- Score

86. What specifically is the problem? Where does it occur? When does it occur? What is its extent?

<--- Score

87. What is out-of-scope initially?
<--- Score

88. What would be the goal or target for a Data Preparation Tools's improvement team?
<--- Score

89. How do you gather Data Preparation Tools requirements?
<--- Score

90. What are the tasks and definitions?
<--- Score

91. Are different versions of process maps needed to account for the different types of inputs?
<--- Score

92. What is the scope of the Data Preparation Tools work?
<--- Score

93. How have you defined all Data Preparation Tools requirements first?
<--- Score

94. What scope do you want your strategy to cover?
<--- Score

95. When is/was the Data Preparation Tools start date?
<--- Score

96. What is the scope of the Data Preparation Tools effort?
<--- Score

97. Has the improvement team collected the 'voice of the customer' (obtained feedback – qualitative and quantitative)?
<--- Score

98. Are accountability and ownership for Data Preparation Tools clearly defined?
<--- Score

99. Is the improvement team aware of the different versions of a process: what they think it is vs. what it actually is vs. what it should be vs. what it could be?
<--- Score

100. Are required metrics defined, what are they?
<--- Score

101. What are the dynamics of the communication plan?
<--- Score

102. Has a Data Preparation Tools requirement not been met?
<--- Score

103. Are customer(s) identified and segmented according to their different needs and requirements?
<--- Score

104. Has a project plan, Gantt chart, or similar been developed/completed?
<--- Score

105. What are the rough order estimates on cost savings/opportunities that Data Preparation Tools

brings?

<--- Score

106. Are task requirements clearly defined?

<--- Score

107. Is scope creep really all bad news?

<--- Score

108. Is the current 'as is' process being followed? If not, what are the discrepancies?

<--- Score

109. Are there any constraints known that bear on the ability to perform Data Preparation Tools work? How is the team addressing them?

<--- Score

110. Do the problem and goal statements meet the SMART criteria (specific, measurable, attainable, relevant, and time-bound)?

<--- Score

111. What information should you gather?

<--- Score

112. Is it clearly defined in and to your organization what you do?

<--- Score

113. Is Data Preparation Tools currently on schedule according to the plan?

<--- Score

114. What constraints exist that might impact the team?

<--- Score

115. What are the record-keeping requirements of Data Preparation Tools activities?
<--- Score

116. Do you have a Data Preparation Tools success story or case study ready to tell and share?
<--- Score

117. Are roles and responsibilities formally defined?
<--- Score

118. Do you have organizational privacy requirements?
<--- Score

119. Is the scope of Data Preparation Tools defined?
<--- Score

120. What critical content must be communicated – who, what, when, where, and how?
<--- Score

121. Does the team have regular meetings?
<--- Score

122. How can the value of Data Preparation Tools be defined?
<--- Score

123. Who are the Data Preparation Tools improvement team members, including Management Leads and Coaches?
<--- Score

124. What is the definition of success?
<--- Score

125. Has/have the customer(s) been identified?
<--- Score

126. When are meeting minutes sent out? Who is on the distribution list?
<--- Score

127. Do you all define Data Preparation Tools in the same way?
<--- Score

128. What are (control) requirements for Data Preparation Tools Information?
<--- Score

129. What are the Data Preparation Tools tasks and definitions?
<--- Score

130. Who is gathering Data Preparation Tools information?
<--- Score

131. Is special Data Preparation Tools user knowledge required?
<--- Score

132. How did the Data Preparation Tools manager receive input to the development of a Data Preparation Tools improvement plan and the estimated completion dates/times of each activity?
<--- Score

Add up total points for this section:
_____ = Total points for this section

Divided by: _____ (number of
statements answered) = _____
Average score for this section

Transfer your score to the Data
Preparation Tools Index at the
beginning of the Self-Assessment.

CRITERION #3: MEASURE:

INTENT: Gather the correct data.
Measure the current performance and
evolution of the situation.

In my belief, the answer to this
question is clearly defined:

5 Strongly Agree

4 Agree

3 Neutral

2 Disagree

1 Strongly Disagree

**1. What details are required of the Data
Preparation Tools cost structure?**
<--- Score

2. Do you have an issue in getting priority?
<--- Score

3. What do people want to verify?
<--- Score

4. What is your decision requirements diagram?
<--- Score

5. What are the current costs of the Data Preparation Tools process?
<--- Score

6. How are measurements made?
<--- Score

7. What relevant entities could be measured?
<--- Score

8. What are the Data Preparation Tools investment costs?
<--- Score

9. How do you aggregate measures across priorities?
<--- Score

10. What tests verify requirements?
<--- Score

11. What is the root cause(s) of the problem?
<--- Score

12. Are you able to realize any cost savings?
<--- Score

13. How can you reduce costs?
<--- Score

14. Are the measurements objective?
<--- Score

15. What is measured? Why?
<--- Score

16. Do you have a flow diagram of what happens?
<--- Score

17. Are missed Data Preparation Tools opportunities costing your organization money?
<--- Score

18. Do you effectively measure and reward individual and team performance?
<--- Score

19. What is the total fixed cost?
<--- Score

20. What causes investor action?
<--- Score

21. What does a Test Case verify?
<--- Score

22. What do you measure and why?
<--- Score

23. What does your operating model cost?
<--- Score

24. How to cause the change?
<--- Score

25. Are there competing Data Preparation Tools priorities?
<--- Score

26. Does the Data Preparation Tools task fit the client's priorities?
<--- Score

27. What potential environmental factors impact the Data Preparation Tools effort?
<--- Score

28. How can you measure the performance?
<--- Score

29. What are your primary costs, revenues, assets?
<--- Score

30. What causes mismanagement?
<--- Score

31. What harm might be caused?
<--- Score

32. How do you verify performance?
<--- Score

33. How do you verify the authenticity of the data and information used?
<--- Score

34. What is an unallowable cost?
<--- Score

35. How will effects be measured?
<--- Score

36. When are costs are incurred?
<--- Score

37. What does losing customers cost your organization?

<--- Score

38. What are the costs?

<--- Score

39. How frequently do you track Data Preparation Tools measures?

<--- Score

40. How can you measure Data Preparation Tools in a systematic way?

<--- Score

41. How do you measure lifecycle phases?

<--- Score

42. What would be a real cause for concern?

<--- Score

43. Which Data Preparation Tools impacts are significant?

<--- Score

44. How do you measure success?

<--- Score

45. What disadvantage does this cause for the user?

<--- Score

46. How do you verify your resources?

<--- Score

47. Do you aggressively reward and promote the

people who have the biggest impact on creating excellent Data Preparation Tools services/products?
<--- Score

48. What are the uncertainties surrounding estimates of impact?
<--- Score

49. Have you made assumptions about the shape of the future, particularly its impact on your customers and competitors?
<--- Score

50. What can be used to verify compliance?
<--- Score

51. Are there any easy-to-implement alternatives to Data Preparation Tools? Sometimes other solutions are available that do not require the cost implications of a full-blown project?
<--- Score

52. How can you reduce the costs of obtaining inputs?
<--- Score

53. What is the cost of rework?
<--- Score

54. What methods are feasible and acceptable to estimate the impact of reforms?
<--- Score

55. How will you measure your Data Preparation Tools effectiveness?
<--- Score

56. How do you prevent mis-estimating cost?
<--- Score

57. What are the estimated costs of proposed changes?
<--- Score

58. Are supply costs steady or fluctuating?
<--- Score

59. Do you have any cost Data Preparation Tools limitation requirements?
<--- Score

60. How do you control the overall costs of your work processes?
<--- Score

61. How do you verify and validate the Data Preparation Tools data?
<--- Score

62. What are the Data Preparation Tools key cost drivers?
<--- Score

63. Did you tackle the cause or the symptom?
<--- Score

64. Which measures and indicators matter?
<--- Score

65. Is there an opportunity to verify requirements?
<--- Score

66. How is progress measured?

<--- Score

67. What could cause delays in the schedule?
<--- Score

68. How much does it cost?
<--- Score

69. Do the benefits outweigh the costs?
<--- Score

70. Among the Data Preparation Tools product and service cost to be estimated, which is considered hardest to estimate?
<--- Score

71. Are there measurements based on task performance?
<--- Score

72. How can a Data Preparation Tools test verify your ideas or assumptions?
<--- Score

73. What are the costs and benefits?
<--- Score

74. Who pays the cost?
<--- Score

75. What are the types and number of measures to use?
<--- Score

76. When a disaster occurs, who gets priority?
<--- Score

77. Why do you expend time and effort to implement measurement, for whom?

<--- Score

78. What drives O&M cost?

<--- Score

79. Have design-to-cost goals been established?

<--- Score

80. Where is the cost?

<--- Score

81. How are costs allocated?

<--- Score

82. At what cost?

<--- Score

83. How will your organization measure success?

<--- Score

84. What are hidden Data Preparation Tools quality costs?

<--- Score

85. Does a Data Preparation Tools quantification method exist?

<--- Score

86. Where is it measured?

<--- Score

87. Have you included everything in your Data Preparation Tools cost models?

<--- Score

88. Is the solution cost-effective?
<--- Score

89. What are your customers expectations and measures?
<--- Score

90. How will costs be allocated?
<--- Score

91. What is the total cost related to deploying Data Preparation Tools, including any consulting or professional services?
<--- Score

92. What causes innovation to fail or succeed in your organization?
<--- Score

93. Are the Data Preparation Tools benefits worth its costs?
<--- Score

94. Who should receive measurement reports?
<--- Score

95. Why do the measurements/indicators matter?
<--- Score

96. What are the operational costs after Data Preparation Tools deployment?
<--- Score

97. Are the units of measure consistent?

<--- Score

98. How sensitive must the Data Preparation Tools strategy be to cost?

<--- Score

99. What causes extra work or rework?

<--- Score

100. How do you measure variability?

<--- Score

101. How will success or failure be measured?

<--- Score

102. How is performance measured?

<--- Score

103. What are the strategic priorities for this year?

<--- Score

104. Are Data Preparation Tools vulnerabilities categorized and prioritized?

<--- Score

105. Has a cost center been established?

<--- Score

106. What measurements are possible, practicable and meaningful?

<--- Score

107. Which costs should be taken into account?

<--- Score

108. Are indirect costs charged to the Data

Preparation Tools program?

<--- Score

109. Is the cost worth the Data Preparation Tools effort ?

<--- Score

110. How do you measure efficient delivery of Data Preparation Tools services?

<--- Score

111. What is the Data Preparation Tools business impact?

<--- Score

112. What users will be impacted?

<--- Score

113. What are allowable costs?

<--- Score

114. How do you verify if Data Preparation Tools is built right?

<--- Score

115. What would it cost to replace your technology?

<--- Score

116. How is the value delivered by Data Preparation Tools being measured?

<--- Score

117. Are actual costs in line with budgeted costs?

<--- Score

118. How will you measure success?
<--- Score

119. How do you quantify and qualify impacts?
<--- Score

120. What are your key Data Preparation Tools organizational performance measures, including key short and longer-term financial measures?
<--- Score

121. What could cause you to change course?
<--- Score

122. What is your Data Preparation Tools quality cost segregation study?
<--- Score

123. When should you bother with diagrams?
<--- Score

124. How do your measurements capture actionable Data Preparation Tools information for use in exceeding your customers expectations and securing your customers engagement?
<--- Score

125. Was a business case (cost/benefit) developed?
<--- Score

126. Are you taking your company in the direction of better and revenue or cheaper and cost?
<--- Score

127. Will Data Preparation Tools have an impact on current business continuity, disaster recovery

processes and/or infrastructure?

<--- Score

128. What measurements are being captured?

<--- Score

129. How do you verify and develop ideas and innovations?

<--- Score

130. What evidence is there and what is measured?

<--- Score

Add up total points for this section:

_ _ _ _ _ = Total points for this section

Divided by: _ _ _ _ _ _ (number of statements answered) = _ _ _ _ _ _ Average score for this section

Transfer your score to the Data Preparation Tools Index at the beginning of the Self-Assessment.

CRITERION #4: ANALYZE:

INTENT: Analyze causes, assumptions
and hypotheses.

In my belief, the answer to this
question is clearly defined:

5 Strongly Agree

4 Agree

3 Neutral

2 Disagree

1 Strongly Disagree

1. Do your employees have the opportunity to do
what they do best everyday?
<--- Score

2. When should a process be art not science?
<--- Score

**3. Who is involved in the management review
process?**
<--- Score

4. Do staff qualifications match your project?
<--- Score

5. What tools were used to generate the list of possible causes?
<--- Score

6. How do you ensure that the Data Preparation Tools opportunity is realistic?
<--- Score

7. Has data output been validated?
<--- Score

8. Has an output goal been set?
<--- Score

9. What data do you need to collect?
<--- Score

10. Do you have the authority to produce the output?
<--- Score

11. How is the Data Preparation Tools Value Stream Mapping managed?
<--- Score

12. What is the output?
<--- Score

13. Where is the data coming from to measure compliance?
<--- Score

14. Is there any way to speed up the process?
<--- Score

15. What is the oversight process?
<--- Score

16. Did any value-added analysis or 'lean thinking' take place to identify some of the gaps shown on the 'as is' process map?
<--- Score

17. What is your organizations process which leads to recognition of value generation?
<--- Score

18. Are all staff in core Data Preparation Tools subjects Highly Qualified?
<--- Score

19. Who gets your output?
<--- Score

20. How do you identify specific Data Preparation Tools investment opportunities and emerging trends?
<--- Score

21. Do you understand your management processes today?
<--- Score

22. What quality tools were used to get through the analyze phase?
<--- Score

23. What does the data say about the performance of the stakeholder process?

<--- Score

24. Did any additional data need to be collected?
<--- Score

25. What controls do you have in place to protect data?
<--- Score

26. How does the organization define, manage, and improve its Data Preparation Tools processes?
<--- Score

27. What tools were used to narrow the list of possible causes?
<--- Score

28. Have you defined which data is gathered how?
<--- Score

29. Is the performance gap determined?
<--- Score

30. What qualifications are needed?
<--- Score

31. Is the required Data Preparation Tools data gathered?
<--- Score

32. How will the Data Preparation Tools data be captured?
<--- Score

33. What are your best practices for minimizing Data Preparation Tools project risk, while demonstrating

incremental value and quick wins throughout the Data Preparation Tools project lifecycle?
<--- Score

34. Think about the functions involved in your Data Preparation Tools project, what processes flow from these functions?
<--- Score

35. Are gaps between current performance and the goal performance identified?
<--- Score

36. What successful thing are you doing today that may be blinding you to new growth opportunities?
<--- Score

37. How often will data be collected for measures?
<--- Score

38. How are outputs preserved and protected?
<--- Score

39. What Data Preparation Tools data should be managed?
<--- Score

40. Were there any improvement opportunities identified from the process analysis?
<--- Score

41. Is the final output clearly identified?
<--- Score

42. Were any designed experiments used to generate additional insight into the data analysis?

<--- Score

43. What qualifications do Data Preparation Tools leaders need?
<--- Score

44. What types of data do your Data Preparation Tools indicators require?
<--- Score

45. What is the cost of poor quality as supported by the team's analysis?
<--- Score

46. What resources go in to get the desired output?
<--- Score

47. What are your current levels and trends in key Data Preparation Tools measures or indicators of product and process performance that are important to and directly serve your customers?
<--- Score

48. How can risk management be tied procedurally to process elements?
<--- Score

49. Is data and process analysis, root cause analysis and quantifying the gap/opportunity in place?
<--- Score

50. Is the Data Preparation Tools process severely broken such that a re-design is necessary?
<--- Score

51. What training and qualifications will you need?

<--- Score

52. How is the way you as the leader think and process information affecting your organizational culture?
<--- Score

53. What other organizational variables, such as reward systems or communication systems, affect the performance of this Data Preparation Tools process?
<--- Score

54. What are the Data Preparation Tools business drivers?
<--- Score

55. How was the detailed process map generated, verified, and validated?
<--- Score

56. What, related to, Data Preparation Tools processes does your organization outsource?
<--- Score

57. How do mission and objectives affect the Data Preparation Tools processes of your organization?
<--- Score

58. What process should you select for improvement?
<--- Score

59. Which Data Preparation Tools data should be retained?
<--- Score

60. How do you define collaboration and team output?

<--- Score

61. Have any additional benefits been identified that will result from closing all or most of the gaps?
<--- Score

62. What conclusions were drawn from the team's data collection and analysis? How did the team reach these conclusions?
<--- Score

63. Who is involved with workflow mapping?
<--- Score

64. Where is Data Preparation Tools data gathered?
<--- Score

65. What data is gathered?
<--- Score

66. Do your leaders quickly bounce back from setbacks?
<--- Score

67. What process improvements will be needed?
<--- Score

68. Is there an established change management process?
<--- Score

69. Do several people in different organizational units assist with the Data Preparation Tools process?
<--- Score

70. How difficult is it to qualify what Data Preparation Tools ROI is?

<--- Score

71. How do your work systems and key work processes relate to and capitalize on your core competencies?

<--- Score

72. How is Data Preparation Tools data gathered?

<--- Score

73. What are your key performance measures or indicators and in-process measures for the control and improvement of your Data Preparation Tools processes?

<--- Score

74. Are Data Preparation Tools changes recognized early enough to be approved through the regular process?

<--- Score

75. What will drive Data Preparation Tools change?

<--- Score

76. Who owns what data?

<--- Score

77. Where can you get qualified talent today?

<--- Score

78. Are all team members qualified for all tasks?

<--- Score

79. What qualifications are necessary?

<--- Score

80. What are the necessary qualifications?
<--- Score

81. What are the revised rough estimates of the financial savings/opportunity for Data Preparation Tools improvements?
<--- Score

82. Is there a strict change management process?
<--- Score

83. What other jobs or tasks affect the performance of the steps in the Data Preparation Tools process?
<--- Score

84. What are the best opportunities for value improvement?
<--- Score

85. Think about some of the processes you undertake within your organization, which do you own?
<--- Score

86. Record-keeping requirements flow from the records needed as inputs, outputs, controls and for transformation of a Data Preparation Tools process, are the records needed as inputs to the Data Preparation Tools process available?
<--- Score

87. What is your organizations system for selecting qualified vendors?
<--- Score

88. How do you measure the operational performance of your key work systems and processes, including productivity, cycle time, and other appropriate measures of process effectiveness, efficiency, and innovation?

<--- Score

89. How many input/output points does it require?

<--- Score

90. An organizationally feasible system request is one that considers the mission, goals and objectives of the organization, key questions are: is the Data Preparation Tools solution request practical and will it solve a problem or take advantage of an opportunity to achieve company goals?

<--- Score

91. How has the Data Preparation Tools data been gathered?

<--- Score

92. What did the team gain from developing a sub-process map?

<--- Score

93. What Data Preparation Tools data should be collected?

<--- Score

94. Do your contracts/agreements contain data security obligations?

<--- Score

95. What were the financial benefits resulting from

any 'ground fruit or low-hanging fruit' (quick fixes)?
<--- Score

96. What systems/processes must you excel at?
<--- Score

97. What are your current levels and trends in key measures or indicators of Data Preparation Tools product and process performance that are important to and directly serve your customers? How do these results compare with the performance of your competitors and other organizations with similar offerings?
<--- Score

98. Are you missing Data Preparation Tools opportunities?
<--- Score

99. Is the suppliers process defined and controlled?
<--- Score

100. Have the problem and goal statements been updated to reflect the additional knowledge gained from the analyze phase?
<--- Score

101. What are your Data Preparation Tools processes?
<--- Score

102. Identify an operational issue in your organization, for example, could a particular task be done more quickly or more efficiently by Data Preparation Tools?
<--- Score

103. Are your outputs consistent?
<--- Score

104. How do you use Data Preparation Tools data and information to support organizational decision making and innovation?
<--- Score

105. What are evaluation criteria for the output?
<--- Score

106. What methods do you use to gather Data Preparation Tools data?
<--- Score

107. What are the processes for audit reporting and management?
<--- Score

108. What do you need to qualify?
<--- Score

109. Who will gather what data?
<--- Score

110. Can you add value to the current Data Preparation Tools decision-making process (largely qualitative) by incorporating uncertainty modeling (more quantitative)?
<--- Score

111. How much data can be collected in the given timeframe?
<--- Score

112. What are the disruptive Data Preparation Tools technologies that enable your organization to radically change your business processes?

<--- Score

113. A compounding model resolution with available relevant data can often provide insight towards a solution methodology; which Data Preparation Tools models, tools and techniques are necessary?

<--- Score

114. Were Pareto charts (or similar) used to portray the 'heavy hitters' (or key sources of variation)?

<--- Score

115. How do you implement and manage your work processes to ensure that they meet design requirements?

<--- Score

116. What is the Data Preparation Tools Driver?

<--- Score

117. Is pre-qualification of suppliers carried out?

<--- Score

118. Do you, as a leader, bounce back quickly from setbacks?

<--- Score

119. Was a detailed process map created to amplify critical steps of the 'as is' stakeholder process?

<--- Score

120. What qualifies as competition?

<--- Score

121. How is the data gathered?
<--- Score

122. How will the change process be managed?
<--- Score

123. Is the gap/opportunity displayed and
communicated in financial terms?
<--- Score

**124. Should you invest in industry-recognized
qualifications?**
<--- Score

125. What were the crucial 'moments of truth' on the
process map?
<--- Score

126. What Data Preparation Tools data do you gather
or use now?
<--- Score

127. What is the complexity of the output produced?
<--- Score

128. What are your outputs?
<--- Score

129. What are the personnel training and
qualifications required?
<--- Score

130. What kind of crime could a potential new hire
have committed that would not only not disqualify

him/her from being hired by your organization, but would actually indicate that he/she might be a particularly good fit?
<--- Score

131. Was a cause-and-effect diagram used to explore the different types of causes (or sources of variation)?
<--- Score

132. What internal processes need improvement?
<--- Score

133. Who qualifies to gain access to data?
<--- Score

134. What output to create?
<--- Score

135. How do you promote understanding that opportunity for improvement is not criticism of the status quo, or the people who created the status quo?
<--- Score

Add up total points for this section:
_ _ _ _ _ = Total points for this section

Divided by: _ _ _ _ _ _ (number of statements answered) = _ _ _ _ _ _
Average score for this section

Transfer your score to the Data Preparation Tools Index at the beginning of the Self-Assessment.

CRITERION #5: IMPROVE:

INTENT: Develop a practical solution. Innovate, establish and test the solution and to measure the results.

In my belief, the answer to this question is clearly defined:

5 Strongly Agree

4 Agree

3 Neutral

2 Disagree

1 Strongly Disagree

1. What risks do you need to manage?
<--- Score

2. How do the Data Preparation Tools results compare with the performance of your competitors and other organizations with similar offerings?
<--- Score

3. Is risk periodically assessed?
<--- Score

4. What are the concrete Data Preparation Tools results?
<--- Score

5. How do you measure progress and evaluate training effectiveness?
<--- Score

6. How does the team improve its work?
<--- Score

7. Is there a high likelihood that any recommendations will achieve their intended results?
<--- Score

8. How do you measure improved Data Preparation Tools service perception, and satisfaction?
<--- Score

9. Are the risks fully understood, reasonable and manageable?
<--- Score

10. How can you improve performance?
<--- Score

11. Is there any other Data Preparation Tools solution?
<--- Score

12. Who are the Data Preparation Tools decision-makers?
<--- Score

13. How is knowledge sharing about risk management improved?
<--- Score

14. What tools were used to tap into the creativity and encourage 'outside the box' thinking?
<--- Score

15. Do you cover the five essential competencies: Communication, Collaboration,Innovation, Adaptability, and Leadership that improve an organizations ability to leverage the new Data Preparation Tools in a volatile global economy?
<--- Score

16. Who will be responsible for documenting the Data Preparation Tools requirements in detail?
<--- Score

17. How will you recognize and celebrate results?
<--- Score

18. What do you want to improve?
<--- Score

19. If you could go back in time five years, what decision would you make differently? What is your best guess as to what decision you're making today you might regret five years from now?
<--- Score

20. Which Data Preparation Tools solution is appropriate?
<--- Score

21. What actually has to improve and by how much?

<--- Score

22. Data Preparation Tools risk decisions: whose call Is It?

<--- Score

23. Which of the recognised risks out of all risks can be most likely transferred?

<--- Score

24. How are Data Preparation Tools risks managed?

<--- Score

25. How do you improve Data Preparation Tools service perception, and satisfaction?

<--- Score

26. What is the team's contingency plan for potential problems occurring in implementation?

<--- Score

27. How do you decide how much to remunerate an employee?

<--- Score

28. Do those selected for the Data Preparation Tools team have a good general understanding of what Data Preparation Tools is all about?

<--- Score

29. What error proofing will be done to address some of the discrepancies observed in the 'as is' process?

<--- Score

30. How can you better manage risk?
<--- Score

31. Can the solution be designed and implemented within an acceptable time period?
<--- Score

32. What tools were most useful during the improve phase?
<--- Score

33. How can you improve Data Preparation Tools?
<--- Score

34. Would you develop a Data Preparation Tools Communication Strategy?
<--- Score

35. Is there a cost/benefit analysis of optimal solution(s)?
<--- Score

36. Who controls key decisions that will be made?
<--- Score

37. How scalable is your Data Preparation Tools solution?
<--- Score

38. Where do you need Data Preparation Tools improvement?
<--- Score

39. Does the goal represent a desired result that can be measured?
<--- Score

40. Is the Data Preparation Tools documentation thorough?

<--- Score

41. Were any criteria developed to assist the team in testing and evaluating potential solutions?

<--- Score

42. How risky is your organization?

<--- Score

43. Can you integrate quality management and risk management?

<--- Score

44. What is the implementation plan?

<--- Score

45. What are the implications of the one critical Data Preparation Tools decision 10 minutes, 10 months, and 10 years from now?

<--- Score

46. How are policy decisions made and where?

<--- Score

47. Is a contingency plan established?

<--- Score

48. Do you combine technical expertise with business knowledge and Data Preparation Tools Key topics include lifecycles, development approaches, requirements and how to make a business case?

<--- Score

49. What are the Data Preparation Tools security risks?
<--- Score

50. Explorations of the frontiers of Data Preparation Tools will help you build influence, improve Data Preparation Tools, optimize decision making, and sustain change, what is your approach?
<--- Score

51. What strategies for Data Preparation Tools improvement are successful?
<--- Score

52. How do you improve productivity?
<--- Score

53. Who controls the risk?
<--- Score

54. When you map the key players in your own work and the types/domains of relationships with them, which relationships do you find easy and which challenging, and why?
<--- Score

55. What improvements have been achieved?
<--- Score

56. Is the implementation plan designed?
<--- Score

57. What area needs the greatest improvement?
<--- Score

58. What attendant changes will need to be made to ensure that the solution is successful?

<--- Score

59. Is the scope clearly documented?

<--- Score

60. What is the Data Preparation Tools's sustainability risk?

<--- Score

61. Is Data Preparation Tools documentation maintained?

<--- Score

62. Who will be responsible for making the decisions to include or exclude requested changes once Data Preparation Tools is underway?

<--- Score

63. Are procedures documented for managing Data Preparation Tools risks?

<--- Score

64. Have you achieved Data Preparation Tools improvements?

<--- Score

65. What alternative responses are available to manage risk?

<--- Score

66. What were the underlying assumptions on the cost-benefit analysis?

<--- Score

67. What to do with the results or outcomes of measurements?

<--- Score

68. What communications are necessary to support the implementation of the solution?
<--- Score

69. How do you keep improving Data Preparation Tools?
<--- Score

70. Was a Data Preparation Tools charter developed?
<--- Score

71. Is supporting Data Preparation Tools documentation required?
<--- Score

72. How is continuous improvement applied to risk management?
<--- Score

73. How do you deal with Data Preparation Tools risk?
<--- Score

74. To what extent does management recognize Data Preparation Tools as a tool to increase the results?
<--- Score

75. Who are the people involved in developing and implementing Data Preparation Tools?
<--- Score

76. Are the most efficient solutions problem-specific?
<--- Score

77. What does the 'should be' process map/design

look like?
<--- Score

78. Why improve in the first place?
<--- Score

79. What are the expected Data Preparation Tools results?
<--- Score

80. What are your current levels and trends in key measures or indicators of workforce and leader development?
<--- Score

81. At what point will vulnerability assessments be performed once Data Preparation Tools is put into production (e.g., ongoing Risk Management after implementation)?
<--- Score

82. Does a good decision guarantee a good outcome?
<--- Score

83. Is there a small-scale pilot for proposed improvement(s)? What conclusions were drawn from the outcomes of a pilot?
<--- Score

84. Is the solution technically practical?
<--- Score

85. Who should make the Data Preparation Tools decisions?
<--- Score

86. How do you improve your likelihood of success ?
<--- Score

87. Was a pilot designed for the proposed solution(s)?
<--- Score

88. Risk Identification: What are the possible risk events your organization faces in relation to Data Preparation Tools?
<--- Score

89. Are risk triggers captured?
<--- Score

90. Risk factors: what are the characteristics of Data Preparation Tools that make it risky?
<--- Score

91. What lessons, if any, from a pilot were incorporated into the design of the full-scale solution?
<--- Score

92. How will you know that you have improved?
<--- Score

93. How will you know when its improved?
<--- Score

94. Risk events: what are the things that could go wrong?
<--- Score

95. What tools were used to evaluate the potential solutions?
<--- Score

96. For decision problems, how do you develop a decision statement?

<--- Score

97. How can skill-level changes improve Data Preparation Tools?

<--- Score

98. What Data Preparation Tools improvements can be made?

<--- Score

99. What tools do you use once you have decided on a Data Preparation Tools strategy and more importantly how do you choose?

<--- Score

100. Who manages supplier risk management in your organization?

<--- Score

101. How do you manage and improve your Data Preparation Tools work systems to deliver customer value and achieve organizational success and sustainability?

<--- Score

102. Do vendor agreements bring new compliance risk ?

<--- Score

103. What were the criteria for evaluating a Data Preparation Tools pilot?

<--- Score

104. How risky is your organization?

<--- Score

105. What should a proof of concept or pilot accomplish?

<--- Score

106. How do you define the solutions' scope?

<--- Score

107. Is the Data Preparation Tools risk managed?

<--- Score

108. What resources are required for the improvement efforts?

<--- Score

109. Who are the Data Preparation Tools decision makers?

<--- Score

110. Are events managed to resolution?

<--- Score

111. What is the magnitude of the improvements?

<--- Score

112. Who are the key stakeholders for the Data Preparation Tools evaluation?

<--- Score

113. Is any Data Preparation Tools documentation required?

<--- Score

114. Is a solution implementation plan established,

including schedule/work breakdown structure, resources, risk management plan, cost/budget, and control plan?

<--- Score

115. Can you identify any significant risks or exposures to Data Preparation Tools third- parties (vendors, service providers, alliance partners etc) that concern you?

<--- Score

116. How will you know that a change is an improvement?

<--- Score

117. What needs improvement? Why?

<--- Score

118. What is Data Preparation Tools's impact on utilizing the best solution(s)?

<--- Score

119. For estimation problems, how do you develop an estimation statement?

<--- Score

120. Who do you report Data Preparation Tools results to?

<--- Score

121. What is Data Preparation Tools risk?

<--- Score

122. Is the optimal solution selected based on testing and analysis?

<--- Score

123. Are you assessing Data Preparation Tools and risk?

<--- Score

124. How do you link measurement and risk?

<--- Score

125. Will the controls trigger any other risks?

<--- Score

126. Do you need to do a usability evaluation?

<--- Score

127. What is the risk?

<--- Score

128. Do you have the optimal project management team structure?

<--- Score

129. How can the phases of Data Preparation Tools development be identified?

<--- Score

130. What current systems have to be understood and/or changed?

<--- Score

131. How do you go about comparing Data Preparation Tools approaches/solutions?

<--- Score

132. Are decisions made in a timely manner?

<--- Score

133. What can you do to improve?
<--- Score

134. Where do the Data Preparation Tools decisions reside?
<--- Score

135. Is pilot data collected and analyzed?
<--- Score

136. What practices helps your organization to develop its capacity to recognize patterns?
<--- Score

137. How significant is the improvement in the eyes of the end user?
<--- Score

138. Who manages Data Preparation Tools risk?
<--- Score

139. Are risk management tasks balanced centrally and locally?
<--- Score

140. Who will be using the results of the measurement activities?
<--- Score

Add up total points for this section:
_ _ _ _ _ = Total points for this section

Divided by: _ _ _ _ _ _ (number of statements answered) = _ _ _ _ _ _
Average score for this section

Transfer your score to the Data
Preparation Tools Index at the
beginning of the Self-Assessment.

CRITERION #6: CONTROL:

INTENT: Implement the practical solution. Maintain the performance and correct possible complications.

In my belief, the answer to this question is clearly defined:

5 Strongly Agree

4 Agree

3 Neutral

2 Disagree

1 Strongly Disagree

1. Is there a standardized process?
<--- Score

2. How do senior leaders actions reflect a commitment to the organizations Data Preparation Tools values?
<--- Score

3. How will the process owner and team be able to

hold the gains?
<--- Score

4. How likely is the current Data Preparation Tools plan to come in on schedule or on budget?
<--- Score

5. Has the improved process and its steps been standardized?
<--- Score

6. Will your goals reflect your program budget?
<--- Score

7. Who controls critical resources?
<--- Score

8. Does Data Preparation Tools appropriately measure and monitor risk?
<--- Score

9. Are you measuring, monitoring and predicting Data Preparation Tools activities to optimize operations and profitability, and enhancing outcomes?
<--- Score

10. How will the day-to-day responsibilities for monitoring and continual improvement be transferred from the improvement team to the process owner?
<--- Score

11. Are the planned controls in place?
<--- Score

12. How will Data Preparation Tools decisions be made and monitored?
<--- Score

13. What is the recommended frequency of auditing?
<--- Score

14. How is Data Preparation Tools project cost planned, managed, monitored?
<--- Score

15. What are the known security controls?
<--- Score

16. Does the Data Preparation Tools performance meet the customer's requirements?
<--- Score

17. Are new process steps, standards, and documentation ingrained into normal operations?
<--- Score

18. Who is going to spread your message?
<--- Score

19. Does a troubleshooting guide exist or is it needed?
<--- Score

20. Is a response plan in place for when the input, process, or output measures indicate an 'out-of-control' condition?
<--- Score

21. How do you establish and deploy modified action plans if circumstances require a shift in plans and rapid execution of new plans?

<--- Score

22. You may have created your quality measures at a time when you lacked resources, technology wasn't up to the required standard, or low service levels were the industry norm. Have those circumstances changed?
<--- Score

23. How will input, process, and output variables be checked to detect for sub-optimal conditions?
<--- Score

24. Who will be in control?
<--- Score

25. Are the Data Preparation Tools standards challenging?
<--- Score

26. What is your plan to assess your security risks?
<--- Score

27. Is reporting being used or needed?
<--- Score

28. Who sets the Data Preparation Tools standards?
<--- Score

29. Do the Data Preparation Tools decisions you make today help people and the planet tomorrow?
<--- Score

30. How will you measure your QA plan's effectiveness?
<--- Score

31. Do you monitor the effectiveness of your Data Preparation Tools activities?
<--- Score

32. Where do ideas that reach policy makers and planners as proposals for Data Preparation Tools strengthening and reform actually originate?
<--- Score

33. Are documented procedures clear and easy to follow for the operators?
<--- Score

34. Is there a transfer of ownership and knowledge to process owner and process team tasked with the responsibilities.
<--- Score

35. What are customers monitoring?
<--- Score

36. Is there documentation that will support the successful operation of the improvement?
<--- Score

37. What key inputs and outputs are being measured on an ongoing basis?
<--- Score

38. Are pertinent alerts monitored, analyzed and distributed to appropriate personnel?
<--- Score

39. Does job training on the documented procedures need to be part of the process team's education and

training?

<--- Score

40. What other areas of the group might benefit from the Data Preparation Tools team's improvements, knowledge, and learning?

<--- Score

41. How might the group capture best practices and lessons learned so as to leverage improvements?

<--- Score

42. Is a response plan established and deployed?

<--- Score

43. Is there a documented and implemented monitoring plan?

<--- Score

44. Are controls in place and consistently applied?

<--- Score

45. How can you best use all of your knowledge repositories to enhance learning and sharing?

<--- Score

46. Has the Data Preparation Tools value of standards been quantified?

<--- Score

47. What are the critical parameters to watch?

<--- Score

48. Is knowledge gained on process shared and institutionalized?

<--- Score

49. Have new or revised work instructions resulted?
<--- Score

50. What are you attempting to measure/monitor?
<--- Score

51. Will existing staff require re-training, for example, to learn new business processes?
<--- Score

52. What should the next improvement project be that is related to Data Preparation Tools?
<--- Score

53. What are the key elements of your Data Preparation Tools performance improvement system, including your evaluation, organizational learning, and innovation processes?
<--- Score

54. Against what alternative is success being measured?
<--- Score

55. How will new or emerging customer needs/requirements be checked/communicated to orient the process toward meeting the new specifications and continually reducing variation?
<--- Score

56. Are there documented procedures?
<--- Score

57. What is the best design framework for Data Preparation Tools organization now that, in a post

industrial-age if the top-down, command and control model is no longer relevant?
<--- Score

58. Do you monitor the Data Preparation Tools decisions made and fine tune them as they evolve?
<--- Score

59. What other systems, operations, processes, and infrastructures (hiring practices, staffing, training, incentives/rewards, metrics/dashboards/scorecards, etc.) need updates, additions, changes, or deletions in order to facilitate knowledge transfer and improvements?
<--- Score

60. What is your theory of human motivation, and how does your compensation plan fit with that view?
<--- Score

61. How do you monitor usage and cost?
<--- Score

62. Who is the Data Preparation Tools process owner?
<--- Score

63. How do you spread information?
<--- Score

64. Will any special training be provided for results interpretation?
<--- Score

65. Is there a control plan in place for sustaining improvements (short and long-term)?

<--- Score

66. Will the team be available to assist members in planning investigations?
<--- Score

67. What should you measure to verify efficiency gains?
<--- Score

68. Do the viable solutions scale to future needs?
<--- Score

69. Are the planned controls working?
<--- Score

70. How widespread is its use?
<--- Score

71. Are suggested corrective/restorative actions indicated on the response plan for known causes to problems that might surface?
<--- Score

72. How will report readings be checked to effectively monitor performance?
<--- Score

73. How is change control managed?
<--- Score

74. What quality tools were useful in the control phase?
<--- Score

75. Is there a Data Preparation Tools Communication

plan covering who needs to get what information when?

<--- Score

76. What do your reports reflect?

<--- Score

77. Can you adapt and adjust to changing Data Preparation Tools situations?

<--- Score

78. What can you control?

<--- Score

79. How do your controls stack up?

<--- Score

80. Is the Data Preparation Tools test/monitoring cost justified?

<--- Score

81. How do you select, collect, align, and integrate Data Preparation Tools data and information for tracking daily operations and overall organizational performance, including progress relative to strategic objectives and action plans?

<--- Score

82. Can support from partners be adjusted?

<--- Score

83. What is the control/monitoring plan?

<--- Score

84. What are your results for key measures or indicators of the accomplishment of your Data

Preparation Tools strategy and action plans, including building and strengthening core competencies?

<--- Score

85. Is new knowledge gained imbedded in the response plan?

<--- Score

86. How do controls support value?

<--- Score

87. How will the process owner verify improvement in present and future sigma levels, process capabilities?

<--- Score

88. Are operating procedures consistent?

<--- Score

89. How do you encourage people to take control and responsibility?

<--- Score

90. What Data Preparation Tools standards are applicable?

<--- Score

91. Does the response plan contain a definite closed loop continual improvement scheme (e.g., plan-do-check-act)?

<--- Score

92. Is there a recommended audit plan for routine surveillance inspections of Data Preparation Tools's gains?

<--- Score

93. What do you stand for--and what are you against?
<--- Score

94. Act/Adjust: What Do you Need to Do Differently?
<--- Score

95. Is there an action plan in case of emergencies?
<--- Score

96. What is the standard for acceptable Data Preparation Tools performance?
<--- Score

97. What are the performance and scale of the Data Preparation Tools tools?
<--- Score

98. What do you measure to verify effectiveness gains?
<--- Score

99. Who has control over resources?
<--- Score

100. How do you plan for the cost of succession?
<--- Score

101. How do you plan on providing proper recognition and disclosure of supporting companies?
<--- Score

Add up total points for this section:
_ _ _ _ _ = Total points for this section

Divided by: _____ (number of
statements answered) = _____
Average score for this section

Transfer your score to the Data
Preparation Tools Index at the
beginning of the Self-Assessment.

CRITERION #7: SUSTAIN:

INTENT: Retain the benefits.

In my belief, the answer to this
question is clearly defined:

5 Strongly Agree

4 Agree

3 Neutral

2 Disagree

1 Strongly Disagree

1. Why should you adopt a Data Preparation Tools framework?
<--- Score

2. How do you govern and fulfill your societal responsibilities?
<--- Score

3. Are all key stakeholders present at all Structured Walkthroughs?
<--- Score

4. What relationships among Data Preparation Tools trends do you perceive?

<--- Score

5. What have been your experiences in defining long range Data Preparation Tools goals?

<--- Score

6. What are strategies for increasing support and reducing opposition?

<--- Score

7. How do you keep records, of what?

<--- Score

8. What is the range of capabilities?

<--- Score

9. Why will customers want to buy your organizations products/services?

<--- Score

10. Which individuals, teams or departments will be involved in Data Preparation Tools?

<--- Score

11. How do you listen to customers to obtain actionable information?

<--- Score

12. What are the challenges?

<--- Score

13. What you are going to do to affect the numbers?

<--- Score

14. Which functions and people interact with the supplier and or customer?
<--- Score

15. What should you stop doing?
<--- Score

16. Do you know who is a friend or a foe?
<--- Score

17. What are the long-term Data Preparation Tools goals?
<--- Score

18. How do you go about securing Data Preparation Tools?
<--- Score

19. Do you know what you are doing? And who do you call if you don't?
<--- Score

20. Is there any existing Data Preparation Tools governance structure?
<--- Score

21. What threat is Data Preparation Tools addressing?
<--- Score

22. Is your strategy driving your strategy? Or is the way in which you allocate resources driving your strategy?
<--- Score

23. Do you have the right capabilities and capacities?
<--- Score

24. Do Data Preparation Tools rules make a reasonable demand on a users capabilities?
<--- Score

25. Why is it important to have senior management support for a Data Preparation Tools project?
<--- Score

26. What is the overall talent health of your organization as a whole at senior levels, and for each organization reporting to a member of the Senior Leadership Team?
<--- Score

27. Which Data Preparation Tools goals are the most important?
<--- Score

28. What are the short and long-term Data Preparation Tools goals?
<--- Score

29. What trophy do you want on your mantle?
<--- Score

30. Why do and why don't your customers like your organization?
<--- Score

31. How will you motivate the stakeholders with the least vested interest?
<--- Score

32. What are your most important goals for the strategic Data Preparation Tools objectives?
<--- Score

33. Are you relevant? Will you be relevant five years from now? Ten?
<--- Score

34. Are you making progress, and are you making progress as Data Preparation Tools leaders?
<--- Score

35. If you got fired and a new hire took your place, what would she do different?
<--- Score

36. What are your personal philosophies regarding Data Preparation Tools and how do they influence your work?
<--- Score

37. How do you stay inspired?
<--- Score

38. Has implementation been effective in reaching specified objectives so far?
<--- Score

39. How do you proactively clarify deliverables and Data Preparation Tools quality expectations?
<--- Score

40. What may be the consequences for the performance of an organization if all stakeholders are not consulted regarding Data Preparation

Tools?

<--- Score

41. What happens when a new employee joins the organization?

<--- Score

42. How do you know if you are successful?

<--- Score

43. What is the estimated value of the project?

<--- Score

44. What one word do you want to own in the minds of your customers, employees, and partners?

<--- Score

45. Whom among your colleagues do you trust, and for what?

<--- Score

46. How can you incorporate support to ensure safe and effective use of Data Preparation Tools into the services that you provide?

<--- Score

47. What happens if you do not have enough funding?

<--- Score

48. Are you changing as fast as the world around you?

<--- Score

49. How will you ensure you get what you expected?

<--- Score

50. How can you negotiate Data Preparation Tools successfully with a stubborn boss, an irate client, or a deceitful coworker?

<--- Score

51. Who is the main stakeholder, with ultimate responsibility for driving Data Preparation Tools forward?

<--- Score

52. Which models, tools and techniques are necessary?

<--- Score

53. What are the barriers to increased Data Preparation Tools production?

<--- Score

54. How are you doing compared to your industry?

<--- Score

55. What is a feasible sequencing of reform initiatives over time?

<--- Score

56. Are your responses positive or negative?

<--- Score

57. Who will provide the final approval of Data Preparation Tools deliverables?

<--- Score

58. Is maximizing Data Preparation Tools protection the same as minimizing Data Preparation Tools loss?

<--- Score

59. Is the Data Preparation Tools organization completing tasks effectively and efficiently?
<--- Score

60. Do you have the right people on the bus?
<--- Score

61. Can you do all this work?
<--- Score

62. Who, on the executive team or the board, has spoken to a customer recently?
<--- Score

63. How do you provide a safe environment -physically and emotionally?
<--- Score

64. How do you accomplish your long range Data Preparation Tools goals?
<--- Score

65. Why should people listen to you?
<--- Score

66. Who are the key stakeholders?
<--- Score

67. Have new benefits been realized?
<--- Score

68. To whom do you add value?
<--- Score

69. Are you maintaining a past–present–future perspective throughout the Data Preparation

Tools discussion?
<--- Score

70. How do you track customer value, profitability or financial return, organizational success, and sustainability?
<--- Score

71. What happens at your organization when people fail?
<--- Score

72. Is a Data Preparation Tools breakthrough on the horizon?
<--- Score

73. What is your question? Why?
<--- Score

74. What trouble can you get into?
<--- Score

75. How likely is it that a customer would recommend your company to a friend or colleague?
<--- Score

76. How do you foster the skills, knowledge, talents, attributes, and characteristics you want to have?
<--- Score

77. Do you see more potential in people than they do in themselves?
<--- Score

78. Ask yourself: how would you do this work if you

only had one staff member to do it?

<--- Score

79. What are you trying to prove to yourself, and how might it be hijacking your life and business success?

<--- Score

80. How do you create buy-in?

<--- Score

81. What management system can you use to leverage the Data Preparation Tools experience, ideas, and concerns of the people closest to the work to be done?

<--- Score

82. Marketing budgets are tighter, consumers are more skeptical, and social media has changed forever the way we talk about Data Preparation Tools, how do you gain traction?

<--- Score

83. What will be the consequences to the stakeholder (financial, reputation etc) if Data Preparation Tools does not go ahead or fails to deliver the objectives?

<--- Score

84. If there were zero limitations, what would you do differently?

<--- Score

85. How do you cross-sell and up-sell your Data Preparation Tools success?

<--- Score

86. What business benefits will Data Preparation Tools goals deliver if achieved?
<--- Score

87. Is your basic point _____ or _____?
<--- Score

88. Think of your Data Preparation Tools project, what are the main functions?
<--- Score

89. In the past year, what have you done (or could you have done) to increase the accurate perception of your company/brand as ethical and honest?
<--- Score

90. What are the gaps in your knowledge and experience?
<--- Score

91. How will you know that the Data Preparation Tools project has been successful?
<--- Score

92. What could happen if you do not do it?
<--- Score

93. What is the overall business strategy?
<--- Score

94. What is the source of the strategies for Data Preparation Tools strengthening and reform?
<--- Score

95. If you find that you havent accomplished one of the goals for one of the steps of the Data Preparation

Tools strategy, what will you do to fix it?

<--- Score

96. What did you miss in the interview for the worst hire you ever made?

<--- Score

97. How do you set Data Preparation Tools stretch targets and how do you get people to not only participate in setting these stretch targets but also that they strive to achieve these?

<--- Score

98. What Data Preparation Tools skills are most important?

<--- Score

99. What are the key enablers to make this Data Preparation Tools move?

<--- Score

100. Instead of going to current contacts for new ideas, what if you reconnected with dormant contacts--the people you used to know? If you were going reactivate a dormant tie, who would it be?

<--- Score

101. What is it like to work for you?

<--- Score

102. How do you manage Data Preparation Tools Knowledge Management (KM)?

<--- Score

103. Were lessons learned captured and

communicated?

<--- Score

104. What are specific Data Preparation Tools rules to follow?

<--- Score

105. Can you break it down?

<--- Score

106. Would you rather sell to knowledgeable and informed customers or to uninformed customers?

<--- Score

107. What would have to be true for the option on the table to be the best possible choice?

<--- Score

108. Do you think Data Preparation Tools accomplishes the goals you expect it to accomplish?

<--- Score

109. What is something you believe that nearly no one agrees with you on?

<--- Score

110. What are the potential basics of Data Preparation Tools fraud?

<--- Score

111. How can you become more high-tech but still be high touch?

<--- Score

112. How do you make it meaningful in connecting Data Preparation Tools with what users do day-to-

day?
<--- Score

113. What is an unauthorized commitment?
<--- Score

114. How do you engage the workforce, in addition to satisfying them?
<--- Score

115. Who is responsible for ensuring appropriate resources (time, people and money) are allocated to Data Preparation Tools?
<--- Score

116. What are the usability implications of Data Preparation Tools actions?
<--- Score

117. Is there a work around that you can use?
<--- Score

118. How long will it take to change?
<--- Score

119. Is a Data Preparation Tools team work effort in place?
<--- Score

120. Who is responsible for Data Preparation Tools?
<--- Score

121. How do senior leaders deploy your organizations vision and values through your leadership system, to the workforce, to key

suppliers and partners, and to customers and other stakeholders, as appropriate?
<--- Score

122. Who are four people whose careers you have enhanced?
<--- Score

123. In retrospect, of the projects that you pulled the plug on, what percent do you wish had been allowed to keep going, and what percent do you wish had ended earlier?
<--- Score

124. If you had to rebuild your organization without any traditional competitive advantages (i.e., no killer technology, promising research, innovative product/service delivery model, etcetera), how would your people have to approach their work and collaborate together in order to create the necessary conditions for success?
<--- Score

125. What must you excel at?
<--- Score

126. Are assumptions made in Data Preparation Tools stated explicitly?
<--- Score

127. What is your BATNA (best alternative to a negotiated agreement)?
<--- Score

128. If your company went out of business tomorrow,

would anyone who doesn't get a paycheck here care?
<--- Score

129. How do you assess the Data Preparation Tools pitfalls that are inherent in implementing it?
<--- Score

130. Whose voice (department, ethnic group, women, older workers, etc) might you have missed hearing from in your company, and how might you amplify this voice to create positive momentum for your business?
<--- Score

131. Are the assumptions believable and achievable?
<--- Score

132. Who will be responsible for deciding whether Data Preparation Tools goes ahead or not after the initial investigations?
<--- Score

133. What counts that you are not counting?
<--- Score

134. What goals did you miss?
<--- Score

135. At what moment would you think; Will I get fired?
<--- Score

136. What are internal and external Data Preparation Tools relations?
<--- Score

137. Who will manage the integration of tools?

<--- Score

138. Who is responsible for errors?
<--- Score

139. What is your Data Preparation Tools strategy?
<--- Score

140. How do you determine the key elements that affect Data Preparation Tools workforce satisfaction, how are these elements determined for different workforce groups and segments?
<--- Score

141. What are the rules and assumptions your industry operates under? What if the opposite were true?
<--- Score

142. How do you lead with Data Preparation Tools in mind?
<--- Score

143. What do we do when new problems arise?
<--- Score

144. Is it economical; do you have the time and money?
<--- Score

145. What was the last experiment you ran?
<--- Score

146. How is implementation research currently incorporated into each of your goals?
<--- Score

147. How can you become the company that would put you out of business?
<--- Score

148. What is the big Data Preparation Tools idea?
<--- Score

149. Do you say no to customers for no reason?
<--- Score

150. What is your competitive advantage?
<--- Score

151. Who will determine interim and final deadlines?
<--- Score

152. Did your employees make progress today?
<--- Score

153. How do customers see your organization?
<--- Score

154. What are current Data Preparation Tools paradigms?
<--- Score

155. What is effective Data Preparation Tools?
<--- Score

156. Political -is anyone trying to undermine this project?
<--- Score

157. What is the purpose of Data Preparation Tools in relation to the mission?
<--- Score

158. Will it be accepted by users?
<--- Score

159. What have you done to protect your business from competitive encroachment?
<--- Score

160. If you weren't already in this business, would you enter it today? And if not, what are you going to do about it?
<--- Score

161. Who are your customers?
<--- Score

162. If no one would ever find out about your accomplishments, how would you lead differently?
<--- Score

163. Are the criteria for selecting recommendations stated?
<--- Score

164. Are there any activities that you can take off your to do list?
<--- Score

165. Can the schedule be done in the given time?
<--- Score

166. How do you transition from the baseline to the target?
<--- Score

167. Do you think you know, or do you know you

know ?
<--- Score

168. Who do you think the world wants your organization to be?
<--- Score

169. What is the kind of project structure that would be appropriate for your Data Preparation Tools project, should it be formal and complex, or can it be less formal and relatively simple?
<--- Score

170. Will there be any necessary staff changes (redundancies or new hires)?
<--- Score

171. How much contingency will be available in the budget?
<--- Score

172. Operational - will it work?
<--- Score

173. Are new benefits received and understood?
<--- Score

174. Are you satisfied with your current role? If not, what is missing from it?
<--- Score

175. How do you maintain Data Preparation Tools's Integrity?
<--- Score

176. What stupid rule would you most like to kill?

<--- Score

177. What potential megatrends could make your business model obsolete?
<--- Score

178. Where can you break convention?
<--- Score

179. How do you deal with Data Preparation Tools changes?
<--- Score

180. Is the impact that Data Preparation Tools has shown?
<--- Score

181. Have benefits been optimized with all key stakeholders?
<--- Score

182. What are the top 3 things at the forefront of your Data Preparation Tools agendas for the next 3 years?
<--- Score

183. Who uses your product in ways you never expected?
<--- Score

184. Who else should you help?
<--- Score

185. What is the funding source for this project?
<--- Score

186. Are you / should you be revolutionary or

evolutionary?
<--- Score

187. Is Data Preparation Tools realistic, or are you setting yourself up for failure?
<--- Score

188. Who have you, as a company, historically been when you've been at your best?
<--- Score

189. Can you maintain your growth without detracting from the factors that have contributed to your success?
<--- Score

190. Who do we want your customers to become?
<--- Score

191. Is Data Preparation Tools dependent on the successful delivery of a current project?
<--- Score

192. Why is Data Preparation Tools important for you now?
<--- Score

193. How do you ensure that implementations of Data Preparation Tools products are done in a way that ensures safety?
<--- Score

194. Do you have past Data Preparation Tools successes?
<--- Score

195. What information is critical to your organization that your executives are ignoring?
<--- Score

196. What are the success criteria that will indicate that Data Preparation Tools objectives have been met and the benefits delivered?
<--- Score

197. What are the essentials of internal Data Preparation Tools management?
<--- Score

198. What is your formula for success in Data Preparation Tools ?
<--- Score

199. What Data Preparation Tools modifications can you make work for you?
<--- Score

200. How will you insure seamless interoperability of Data Preparation Tools moving forward?
<--- Score

201. What unique value proposition (UVP) do you offer?
<--- Score

202. When information truly is ubiquitous, when reach and connectivity are completely global, when computing resources are infinite, and when a whole new set of impossibilities are not only possible, but happening, what will that do to your business?
<--- Score

203. Do you have enough freaky customers in your portfolio pushing you to the limit day in and day out?

<--- Score

204. Are you using a design thinking approach and integrating Innovation, Data Preparation Tools Experience, and Brand Value?

<--- Score

205. What are the business goals Data Preparation Tools is aiming to achieve?

<--- Score

206. How do you keep the momentum going?

<--- Score

207. What knowledge, skills and characteristics mark a good Data Preparation Tools project manager?

<--- Score

208. Who do you want your customers to become?

<--- Score

209. What would you recommend your friend do if he/she were facing this dilemma?

<--- Score

210. What new services of functionality will be implemented next with Data Preparation Tools ?

<--- Score

211. How does Data Preparation Tools integrate with other stakeholder initiatives?

<--- Score

212. If you had to leave your organization for a year and the only communication you could have with employees/colleagues was a single paragraph, what would you write?
<--- Score

213. If you were responsible for initiating and implementing major changes in your organization, what steps might you take to ensure acceptance of those changes?
<--- Score

214. What is the recommended frequency of auditing?
<--- Score

215. If your customer were your grandmother, would you tell her to buy what you're selling?
<--- Score

Add up total points for this section:
_ _ _ _ _ = Total points for this section

Divided by: _ _ _ _ _ _ (number of statements answered) = _ _ _ _ _ _ Average score for this section

Transfer your score to the Data Preparation Tools Index at the beginning of the Self-Assessment.

Data Preparation Tools and Managing Projects, Criteria for Project Managers:

1.0 Initiating Process Group: Data Preparation Tools

1. Mitigate. what will you do to minimize the impact should the risk event occur?

2. How well did you do?

3. Which six sigma dmaic phase focuses on why and how defects and errors occur?

4. What communication items need improvement?

5. What must be done?

6. Are the changes in your Data Preparation Tools project being formally requested, analyzed, and approved by the appropriate decision makers?

7. What areas were overlooked on this Data Preparation Tools project?

8. What is the stake of others in your Data Preparation Tools project?

9. Who are the Data Preparation Tools project stakeholders?

10. During which stage of Risk planning are risks prioritized based on probability and impact?

11. The process to Manage Stakeholders is part of which process group?

12. In which Data Preparation Tools project

management process group is the detailed Data Preparation Tools project budget created?

13. What are the tools and techniques to be used in each phase?

14. Did the Data Preparation Tools project team have the right skills?

15. What business situation is being addressed?

16. What were things that you did well, and could improve, and how?

17. Do you know the roles & responsibilities required for this Data Preparation Tools project?

18. Are you properly tracking the progress of the Data Preparation Tools project and communicating the status to stakeholders?

19. Who is behind the Data Preparation Tools project?

20. Have the stakeholders identified all individual requirements pertaining to business process?

1.1 Project Charter: Data Preparation Tools

21. What outcome, in measureable terms, are you hoping to accomplish?

22. Where does all this information come from?

23. What is the business need?

24. Data Preparation Tools project deliverables: what is the Data Preparation Tools project going to produce?

25. Success determination factors: how will the success of the Data Preparation Tools project be determined from the customers perspective?

26. For whom?

27. Why is it important?

28. Why have you chosen the aim you have set forth?

29. Name and describe the elements that deal with providing the detail?

30. What are the known stakeholder requirements?

31. What are the deliverables?

32. Must Have?

33. What date will the task finish?

34. Who ise input and support will this Data Preparation Tools project require?

35. Why executive support?

36. Who are the stakeholders?

37. What ideas do you have for initial tests of change (PDSA cycles)?

38. What are the assumptions?

39. Who is the Data Preparation Tools project Manager?

40. How high should you set your goals?

1.2 Stakeholder Register: Data Preparation Tools

41. What is the power of the stakeholder?

42. Is your organization ready for change?

43. What are the major Data Preparation Tools project milestones requiring communications or providing communications opportunities?

44. Who wants to talk about Security?

45. How will reports be created?

46. What & Why?

47. How big is the gap?

48. What opportunities exist to provide communications?

49. How much influence do they have on the Data Preparation Tools project?

50. How should employers make voices heard?

51. Who is managing stakeholder engagement?

1.3 Stakeholder Analysis Matrix: Data Preparation Tools

52. What do people from other organizations see as your strengths?

53. How affected by the problem(s)?

54. What unique or lowest-cost resources does the Data Preparation Tools project have access to?

55. Competitive advantages?

56. Cashflow, start-up cash-drain?

57. Partnerships, agencies, distribution?

58. Inoculations or payment to receive them?

59. Who has not been involved up to now and should have been?

60. Reliability of data, plan predictability?

61. Would it be fair to say that cost is a controlling criteria?

62. What is accountability in relation to the Data Preparation Tools project?

63. Who will be affected by the Data Preparation Tools project?

64. Timescales, deadlines and pressures?

65. Vital contracts and partners?

66. How do you manage Data Preparation Tools project Risk?

67. Seasonality, weather effects?

68. Global influences?

69. Could any of your organizations weaknesses seriously threaten development?

70. Who is most dependent on the resources at stake?

71. How to involve media?

2.0 Planning Process Group: Data Preparation Tools

72. Did the program design/ implementation strategy adequately address the planning stage necessary to set up structures, hire staff etc.?

73. What are the different approaches to building the WBS?

74. How should needs be met?

75. How are it Data Preparation Tools projects different?

76. How well do the team follow the chosen processes?

77. Product breakdown structure (pbs): what is the Data Preparation Tools project result or product, and how should it look like, what are its parts?

78. Who are the Data Preparation Tools project stakeholders?

79. To what extent do the intervention objectives and strategies of the Data Preparation Tools project respond to your organizations plans?

80. In what way has the Data Preparation Tools project come up with innovative measures for problem-solving?

81. Are the necessary foundations in place to ensure the sustainability of the results of the Data Preparation Tools project?

82. How will you know you did it?

83. How can you make your needs known?

84. What input will you be required to provide the Data Preparation Tools project team?

85. To what extent has a PMO contributed to raising the quality of the design of the Data Preparation Tools project?

86. Is the identification of the problems, inequalities and gaps, with respective causes, clear in the Data Preparation Tools project?

87. On which process should team members spend the most time?

88. Is the duration of the program sufficient to ensure a cycle that will Data Preparation Tools project the sustainability of the interventions?

89. What will you do?

90. The Data Preparation Tools project charter is created in which Data Preparation Tools project management process group?

91. How do you integrate Data Preparation Tools project Planning with the Iterative/Evolutionary SDLC?

2.1 Project Management Plan: Data Preparation Tools

92. If the Data Preparation Tools project management plan is a comprehensive document that guides you in Data Preparation Tools project execution and control, then what should it NOT contain?

93. Are calculations and results of analyzes essentially correct?

94. Is mitigation authorized or recommended?

95. What did not work so well?

96. What goes into your Data Preparation Tools project Charter?

97. Why Change?

98. What if, for example, the positive direction and vision of your organization causes expected trends to change resulting in greater need than expected?

99. Does the implementation plan have an appropriate division of responsibilities?

100. Do there need to be organizational changes?

101. What worked well?

102. Are the existing and future without-plan conditions reasonable and appropriate?

103. Is the appropriate plan selected based on your organizations objectives and evaluation criteria expressed in Principles and Guidelines policies?

104. Did the planning effort collaborate to develop solutions that integrate expertise, policies, programs, and Data Preparation Tools projects across entities?

105. What is risk management?

106. When is the Data Preparation Tools project management plan created?

107. Are there any windfall benefits that would accrue to the Data Preparation Tools project sponsor or other parties?

108. What is Data Preparation Tools project scope management?

109. What went right?

110. When is a Data Preparation Tools project management plan created?

111. Are there any Client staffing expectations?

2.2 Scope Management Plan: Data Preparation Tools

112. Are internal Data Preparation Tools project status meetings held at reasonable intervals?

113. Are funding resource estimates sufficiently detailed and documented for use in planning and tracking the Data Preparation Tools project?

114. Are there checklists created to demine if all quality processes are followed?

115. Are changes in deliverable commitments agreed to by all affected groups & individuals?

116. Do all stakeholders know how to access this repository and where to find the Data Preparation Tools project documentation?

117. Which statement about customer expectations is not true?

118. Is there an issues management plan in place?

119. Have Data Preparation Tools project management standards and procedures been identified / established and documented?

120. Given the scope of the Data Preparation Tools project, which criterion should be optimized?

121. Have the personnel with the necessary skills and

competence been identified and has agreement for participation in the Data Preparation Tools project been reached with the appropriate management?

122. Does the business case include how the Data Preparation Tools project aligns with your organizations strategic goals & objectives?

123. Have the key functions and capabilities been defined and assigned to each release or iteration?

124. How difficult will it be to do specific activities on this Data Preparation Tools project?

125. Is there a formal set of procedures supporting Issues Management?

126. Organizational policies that might affect the availability of resources?

127. Is the Data Preparation Tools project status reviewed with the steering and executive teams at appropriate intervals?

128. Why is a scope management plan important?

129. Quality standards - are controls in place to ensure that the work was not only completed and also completed to meet specific standards?

2.3 Requirements Management Plan: Data Preparation Tools

130. Who is responsible for monitoring and tracking the Data Preparation Tools project requirements?

131. Has the requirements team been instructed in the Change Control process?

132. Do you have an agreed upon process for alerting the Data Preparation Tools project Manager if a request for change in requirements leads to a product scope change?

133. Are actual resources expenditures versus planned expenditures acceptable?

134. Who will do the reporting and to whom will reports be delivered?

135. How knowledgeable is the primary Stakeholder(s) in the proposed application area?

136. What cost metrics will be used?

137. Who has the authority to reject Data Preparation Tools project requirements?

138. Did you provide clear and concise specifications?

139. Is stakeholder risk tolerance an important factor for the requirements process in this Data Preparation Tools project?

140. Do you have price sheets and a methodology for determining the total proposal cost?

141. Will the product release be stable and mature enough to be deployed in the user community?

142. Will the contractors involved take full responsibility?

143. Describe the process for rejecting the Data Preparation Tools project requirements. Who has the authority to reject Data Preparation Tools project requirements?

144. Do you really need to write this document at all?

145. How detailed should the Data Preparation Tools project get?

146. In case of software development; Should you have a test for each code module?

147. What is the earliest finish date for this Data Preparation Tools project if it is scheduled to start on ...?

148. Will you use an assessment of the Data Preparation Tools project environment as a tool to discover risk to the requirements process?

2.4 Requirements Documentation: Data Preparation Tools

149. Where do system and software requirements come from, what are sources?

150. How much does requirements engineering cost?

151. What facilities must be supported by the system?

152. How does the proposed Data Preparation Tools project contribute to the overall objectives of your organization?

153. How will the proposed Data Preparation Tools project help?

154. What is effective documentation?

155. How does what is being described meet the business need?

156. Who provides requirements?

157. How will requirements be documented and who signs off on them?

158. Has requirements gathering uncovered information that would necessitate changes?

159. What kind of entity is a problem ?

160. How much testing do you need to do to prove

that your system is safe?

161. What will be the integration problems?

162. Basic work/business process; high-level, what is being touched?

163. Where are business rules being captured?

164. Is the origin of the requirement clearly stated?

165. Do technical resources exist?

166. Can you check system requirements?

167. What marketing channels do you want to use: e-mail, letter or sms?

168. Do your constraints stand?

2.5 Requirements Traceability Matrix: Data Preparation Tools

169. Do you have a clear understanding of all subcontracts in place?

170. Why use a WBS?

171. What are the chronologies, contingencies, consequences, criteria?

172. How will it affect the stakeholders personally in career?

173. Why do you manage scope?

174. What percentage of Data Preparation Tools projects are producing traceability matrices between requirements and other work products?

175. Describe the process for approving requirements so they can be added to the traceability matrix and Data Preparation Tools project work can be performed. Will the Data Preparation Tools project requirements become approved in writing?

176. Will you use a Requirements Traceability Matrix?

177. Is there a requirements traceability process in place?

178. What is the WBS?

179. How small is small enough?

180. How do you manage scope?

2.6 Project Scope Statement: Data Preparation Tools

181. Is there a process (test plans, inspections, reviews) defined for verifying outputs for each task?

182. Are there completion/verification criteria defined for each task producing an output?

183. Will there be a Change Control Process in place?

184. Will you need a statement of work?

185. What are the possible consequences should a risk come to occur?

186. What is a process you might recommend to verify the accuracy of the research deliverable?

187. Were potential customers involved early in the planning process?

188. Does the scope statement still need some clarity?

189. Will all tasks resulting from issues be entered into the Data Preparation Tools project Plan and tracked through the plan?

190. Is this process communicated to the customer and team members?

191. Write a brief purpose statement for this Data Preparation Tools project. Include a business

justification statement. What is the product of this Data Preparation Tools project?

192. What is change?

193. Is there a baseline plan against which to measure progress?

194. Is the Data Preparation Tools project organization documented and on file?

195. Have you been able to easily identify success criteria and create objective measurements for each of the Data Preparation Tools project scopes goal statements?

196. Are the meetings set up to have assigned note takers that will add action/issues to the issue list?

197. Are the input requirements from the team members clearly documented and communicated?

198. Did your Data Preparation Tools project ask for this?

199. Is there an information system for the Data Preparation Tools project?

2.7 Assumption and Constraint Log: Data Preparation Tools

200. Does a documented Data Preparation Tools project organizational policy & plan (i.e. governance model) exist?

201. Is there adequate stakeholder participation for the vetting of requirements definition, changes and management?

202. Have the scope, objectives, costs, benefits and impacts been communicated to all involved and/or impacted stakeholders and work groups?

203. Is the definition of the Data Preparation Tools project scope clear; what needs to be accomplished?

204. Have Data Preparation Tools project management standards and procedures been established and documented?

205. How are new requirements or changes to requirements identified?

206. Is staff trained on the software technologies that are being used on the Data Preparation Tools project?

207. After observing execution of process, is it in compliance with the documented Plan?

208. What to do at recovery?

209. Are there nonconformance issues?

210. What do you log?

211. Are there processes defining how software will be developed including development methods, overall timeline for development, software product standards, and traceability?

212. Have adequate resources been provided by management to ensure Data Preparation Tools project success?

213. Are you meeting your customers expectations consistently?

214. When can log be discarded?

215. No superfluous information or marketing narrative?

216. Violation trace: why ?

217. Is there a Steering Committee in place?

218. How relevant is this attribute to this Data Preparation Tools project or audit?

219. What strengths do you have?

2.8 Work Breakdown Structure: Data Preparation Tools

220. Is it a change in scope?

221. Do you need another level?

222. What is the probability that the Data Preparation Tools project duration will exceed xx weeks?

223. When do you stop?

224. Who has to do it?

225. Can you make it?

226. Why would you develop a Work Breakdown Structure?

227. What is the probability of completing the Data Preparation Tools project in less that xx days?

228. How big is a work-package?

229. Is it still viable?

230. How will you and your Data Preparation Tools project team define the Data Preparation Tools projects scope and work breakdown structure?

231. How much detail?

232. How far down?

233. Where does it take place?

234. When does it have to be done?

235. What has to be done?

236. Is the work breakdown structure (wbs) defined and is the scope of the Data Preparation Tools project clear with assigned deliverable owners?

237. When would you develop a Work Breakdown Structure?

238. Why is it useful?

2.9 WBS Dictionary: Data Preparation Tools

239. Are the requirements for all items of overhead established by rational, traceable processes?

240. Is the anticipated (firm and potential) business base Data Preparation Tools projected in a rational, consistent manner?

241. Does the contractors system include procedures for measuring performance of the lowest level organization responsible for the control account?

242. Changes in the nature of the overhead requirements?

243. Are the overhead pools formally and adequately identified?

244. Is all budget available as management reserve identified and excluded from the performance measurement baseline?

245. Do work packages consist of discrete tasks which are adequately described?

246. Does the contractors system provide for determination of price variance by comparing planned Vs actual commitments?

247. The wbs is developed as part of a joint planning session. and how do you know that youhave done this

right?

248. Should you include sub-activities?

249. The Data Preparation Tools projected business base for each period?

250. Changes in the overhead pool and/or organization structures?

251. Are work packages reasonably short in time duration or do they have adequate objective indicators/milestones to minimize subjectivity of the in process work evaluation?

252. Incurrence of actual indirect costs in excess of budgets, by element of expense?

253. Does the contractor have procedures which permit identification of recurring or non-recurring costs as necessary?

254. Budgets assigned to major functional organizations?

255. Are all elements of indirect expense identified to overhead cost budgets of Data Preparation Tools projections?

256. Are detailed work packages planned as far in advance as practicable?

257. Are records maintained to show how management reserves are used?

258. Are all affected work authorizations, budgeting,

and scheduling documents amended to properly reflect the effects of authorized changes?

2.10 Schedule Management Plan: Data Preparation Tools

259. Are risk triggers captured?

260. Is stakeholder involvement adequate?

261. Have all team members been part of identifying risks?

262. Will rolling way planning be used?

263. Are the people assigned to the Data Preparation Tools project sufficiently qualified?

264. Has a capability assessment been conducted?

265. Is documentation created for communication with the suppliers and Vendors?

266. Why time management?

267. Has the schedule been baselined?

268. Staffing Requirements?

269. Are the quality tools and methods identified in the Quality Plan appropriate to the Data Preparation Tools project?

270. Alignment to strategic goals & objectives?

271. Are the Data Preparation Tools project plans

updated on a frequent basis?

272. Has the business need been clearly defined?

273. Are meeting minutes captured and sent out after the meeting?

274. Which status reports are received per the Data Preparation Tools project Plan?

275. Is the plan consistent with industry best practices?

276. Does the resource management plan include a personnel development plan?

277. What happens if a warning is triggered?

2.11 Activity List: Data Preparation Tools

278. Is infrastructure setup part of your Data Preparation Tools project?

279. What is your organizations history in doing similar activities?

280. How detailed should a Data Preparation Tools project get?

281. Is there anything planned that does not need to be here?

282. In what sequence?

283. Can you determine the activity that must finish, before this activity can start?

284. Where will it be performed?

285. Who will perform the work?

286. When do the individual activities need to start and finish?

287. For other activities, how much delay can be tolerated?

288. What is the total time required to complete the Data Preparation Tools project if no delays occur?

289. How much slack is available in the Data Preparation Tools project?

290. How do you determine the late start (LS) for each activity?

291. How will it be performed?

292. What did not go as well?

293. When will the work be performed?

294. What are the critical bottleneck activities?

2.12 Activity Attributes: Data Preparation Tools

295. How difficult will it be to complete specific activities on this Data Preparation Tools project?

296. Are the required resources available or need to be acquired?

297. How do you manage time?

298. Which method produces the more accurate cost assignment?

299. Does your organization of the data change its meaning?

300. Activity: what is In the Bag?

301. Activity: what is Missing?

302. How many resources do you need to complete the work scope within a limit of X number of days?

303. What is the general pattern here?

304. Would you consider either of corresponding activities an outlier?

305. Time for overtime?

306. What went wrong?

307. How many days do you need to complete the work scope with a limit of X number of resources?

308. Resource is assigned to?

309. Can you re-assign any activities to another resource to resolve an over-allocation?

310. Have constraints been applied to the start and finish milestones for the phases?

311. Do you feel very comfortable with your prediction?

312. Where else does it apply?

2.13 Milestone List: Data Preparation Tools

313. Loss of key staff?

314. Usps (unique selling points)?

315. Gaps in capabilities?

316. What would happen if a delivery of material was one week late?

317. How soon can the activity start?

318. Environmental effects?

319. Political effects?

320. How will the milestone be verified?

321. Own known vulnerabilities?

322. How late can the activity start?

323. What has been done so far?

324. Marketing - reach, distribution, awareness?

325. Identify critical paths (one or more) and which activities are on the critical path?

326. It is to be a narrative text providing the crucial aspects of your Data Preparation Tools project

proposal answering what, who, how, when and where?

327. How late can the activity finish?

328. Effects on core activities, distraction?

329. Level of the Innovation?

2.14 Network Diagram: Data Preparation Tools

330. What are the Key Success Factors?

331. If x is long, what would be the completion time if you break x into two parallel parts of y weeks and z weeks?

332. Planning: who, how long, what to do?

333. How difficult will it be to do specific activities on this Data Preparation Tools project?

334. What job or jobs could run concurrently?

335. What controls the start and finish of a job?

336. What is the completion time?

337. Review the logical flow of the network diagram. Take a look at which activities you have first and then sequence the activities. Do they make sense?

338. What activities must follow this activity?

339. What is the probability of completing the Data Preparation Tools project in less that xx days?

340. Which type of network diagram allows you to depict four types of dependencies?

341. What job or jobs follow it?

342. Will crashing x weeks return more in benefits than it costs?

343. Exercise: what is the probability that the Data Preparation Tools project duration will exceed xx weeks?

344. Are you on time?

345. What must be completed before an activity can be started?

346. Where do you schedule uncertainty time?

347. What job or jobs precede it?

348. What activity must be completed immediately before this activity can start?

2.15 Activity Resource Requirements: Data Preparation Tools

349. Organizational Applicability?

350. Which logical relationship does the PDM use most often?

351. When does monitoring begin?

352. How many signatures do you require on a check and does this match what is in your policy and procedures?

353. Other support in specific areas?

354. How do you handle petty cash?

355. Do you use tools like decomposition and rolling-wave planning to produce the activity list and other outputs?

356. Anything else?

357. Are there unresolved issues that need to be addressed?

358. Why do you do that?

359. What are constraints that you might find during the Human Resource Planning process?

360. What is the Work Plan Standard?

2.16 Resource Breakdown Structure: Data Preparation Tools

361. How can this help you with team building?

362. Who is allowed to perform which functions?

363. Which resource planning tool provides information on resource responsibility and accountability?

364. Who delivers the information?

365. Who is allowed to see what data about which resources?

366. What is the primary purpose of the human resource plan?

367. When do they need the information?

368. Are the required resources available?

369. What is the difference between % Complete and % work?

370. Who will use the system?

371. Why do you do it?

372. Changes based on input from stakeholders?

373. Which resources should be in the resource pool?

374. Any changes from stakeholders?

375. Who will be used as a Data Preparation Tools project team member?

2.17 Activity Duration Estimates: Data Preparation Tools

376. If the optimiztic estimate for an activity is 12days, and the pessimistic estimate is 18days, what is the standard deviation of this activity?

377. Account for the four frames of organizations. How can they help Data Preparation Tools project managers understand your organizational context for Data Preparation Tools projects?

378. Are operational definitions created to identify quality measurement criteria for specific activities?

379. Are the causes of all variances identified?

380. Are expert judgment and historical information utilized to estimate activity duration?

381. Do scope statements include the Data Preparation Tools project objectives and expected deliverables?

382. Why do you think schedule issues often cause the most conflicts on Data Preparation Tools projects?

383. What is the critical path for this Data Preparation Tools project and how long is it?

384. What is involved in the solicitation process?

385. Will new hardware or software be required for

servers or client machines?

386. After how many days will the lease cost be the same as the purchase cost for the equipment?

387. Which includes asking team members about the time estimates for activities and reaching agreement on the calendar date for each activity?

388. Is earned value analysis completed to assess Data Preparation Tools project performance?

389. Will additional funds be needed for hardware or software?

390. How does Data Preparation Tools project integration management relate to the Data Preparation Tools project life cycle, stakeholders, and the other Data Preparation Tools project management knowledge areas?

391. Does a process exist for approving or rejecting changes?

392. Will it help in finding or retaining employees?

393. Are activity dependencies documented?

394. Data Preparation Tools project manager has received activity duration estimates from his team. Which does one need in order to complete schedule development?

2.18 Duration Estimating Worksheet: Data Preparation Tools

395. What utility impacts are there?

396. Do any colleagues have experience with your organization and/or RFPs?

397. Small or large Data Preparation Tools project?

398. Is the Data Preparation Tools project responsive to community need?

399. What work will be included in the Data Preparation Tools project?

400. Define the work as completely as possible. What work will be included in the Data Preparation Tools project?

401. Science = process: remember the scientific method?

402. Can the Data Preparation Tools project be constructed as planned?

403. Will the Data Preparation Tools project collaborate with the local community and leverage resources?

404. What is the total time required to complete the Data Preparation Tools project if no delays occur?

405. Why estimate time and cost?

406. Does the Data Preparation Tools project provide innovative ways for stakeholders to overcome obstacles or deliver better outcomes?

407. When does your organization expect to be able to complete it?

408. Is this operation cost effective?

409. When, then?

2.19 Project Schedule: Data Preparation Tools

410. How does a Data Preparation Tools project get to be a year late ?

411. Are quality inspections and review activities listed in the Data Preparation Tools project schedule(s)?

412. Why or why not?

413. Is infrastructure setup part of your Data Preparation Tools project?

414. What documents, if any, will the subcontractor provide (eg Data Preparation Tools project schedule, quality plan etc)?

415. What is the difference?

416. Is Data Preparation Tools project work proceeding in accordance with the original Data Preparation Tools project schedule?

417. Does the condition or event threaten the Data Preparation Tools projects objectives in any ways?

418. To what degree is do you feel the entire team was committed to the Data Preparation Tools project schedule?

419. What are you counting on?

420. Did the Data Preparation Tools project come in under budget?

421. Are there activities that came from a template or previous Data Preparation Tools project that are not applicable on this phase of this Data Preparation Tools project?

422. How much slack is available in the Data Preparation Tools project?

423. Should you have a test for each code module?

424. Did the final product meet or exceed user expectations?

425. Change management required?

426. How can you fix it?

2.20 Cost Management Plan: Data Preparation Tools

427. The definition of the Data Preparation Tools project scope what needs to be accomplished?

428. Is the structure for tracking the Data Preparation Tools project schedule well defined and assigned to a specific individual?

429. Planning and scheduling responsibilities – How will the responsibilities for planning and scheduling be allocated?

430. Are Data Preparation Tools project contact logs kept up to date?

431. Do Data Preparation Tools project teams & team members report on status / activities / progress?

432. What is the work breakdown structure for the Data Preparation Tools project?

433. Are Data Preparation Tools project team members committed fulltime?

434. What is Data Preparation Tools project management?

435. Have the reasons why the changes to your organizational systems and capabilities are required?

436. Is pert / critical path or equivalent methodology

being used?

437. Is there an on-going process in place to monitor Data Preparation Tools project risks?

438. Is the schedule updated on a periodic basis?

439. How does the proposed individual meet each requirement?

440. Risk Analysis?

441. Are changes in scope (deliverable commitments) agreed to by all affected groups & individuals?

442. Are corrective actions and variances reported?

443. Pareto diagrams, statistical sampling, flow charting or trend analysis used quality monitoring?

444. Cost tracking and performance analysis – How will cost tracking and performance analysis be accomplished?

445. Have activity relationships and interdependencies within tasks been adequately identified?

446. Is Data Preparation Tools project work proceeding in accordance with the original Data Preparation Tools project schedule?

2.21 Activity Cost Estimates: Data Preparation Tools

447. Were decisions made in a timely manner?

448. Eac -estimate at completion, what is the total job expected to cost?

449. Review – what are some common errors in activities to avoid?

450. The impact and what actions were taken?

451. Does the estimator estimate by task or by person?

452. Does the activity rely on a common set of tools to carry it out?

453. What is the activity inventory?

454. How do you allocate indirect costs to activities?

455. Which contract type places the most risk on the seller?

456. Are data needed on characteristics of care?

457. Where can you get activity reports?

458. Who & what determines the need for contracted services?

459. What is the Data Preparation Tools projects sustainability strategy that will ensure Data Preparation Tools project results will endure or be sustained?

460. How do you manage cost?

461. Measurable - are the targets measurable?

462. Is there anything unique in this Data Preparation Tools projects scope statement that will affect resources?

463. What were things that you need to improve?

464. How do you fund change orders?

2.22 Cost Estimating Worksheet: Data Preparation Tools

465. What can be included?

466. What will others want?

467. Who is best positioned to know and assist in identifying corresponding factors?

468. What is the estimated labor cost today based upon this information?

469. Value pocket identification & quantification what are value pockets?

470. Will the Data Preparation Tools project collaborate with the local community and leverage resources?

471. What is the purpose of estimating?

472. How will the results be shared and to whom?

473. Does the Data Preparation Tools project provide innovative ways for stakeholders to overcome obstacles or deliver better outcomes?

474. What additional Data Preparation Tools project(s) could be initiated as a result of this Data Preparation Tools project?

475. Identify the timeframe necessary to monitor

progress and collect data to determine how the selected measure has changed?

476. Ask: are others positioned to know, are others credible, and will others cooperate?

477. What happens to any remaining funds not used?

478. Is it feasible to establish a control group arrangement?

479. Is the Data Preparation Tools project responsive to community need?

480. Can a trend be established from historical performance data on the selected measure and are the criteria for using trend analysis or forecasting methods met?

481. What info is needed?

482. What costs are to be estimated?

2.23 Cost Baseline: Data Preparation Tools

483. Is the cr within Data Preparation Tools project scope?

484. What deliverables come first?

485. Has the Data Preparation Tools project documentation been archived or otherwise disposed as described in the Data Preparation Tools project communication plan?

486. What threats might prevent you from getting there?

487. Are you asking management for something as a result of this update?

488. Vac -variance at completion, how much over/under budget do you expect to be?

489. Has the Data Preparation Tools projected annual cost to operate and maintain the product(s) or service(s) been approved and funded?

490. Is there anything you need from upper management in order to be successful?

491. Who will use corresponding metrics ?

492. How fast?

493. Has the Data Preparation Tools project (or Data Preparation Tools project phase) been evaluated against each objective established in the product description and Integrated Data Preparation Tools project Plan?

494. Have the actual milestone completion dates been compared to the approved schedule?

495. Does the suggested change request seem to represent a necessary enhancement to the product?

496. Escalation criteria met?

497. For what purpose ?

498. Data Preparation Tools project goals -should others be reconsidered?

499. Has the appropriate access to relevant data and analysis capability been granted?

500. Has training and knowledge transfer of the operations organization been completed?

2.24 Quality Management Plan: Data Preparation Tools

501. What is the Quality Management Plan?

502. What are your organizations current levels and trends for the already stated measures related to employee wellbeing, satisfaction, and development?

503. Documented results available?

504. How do senior leaders create and communicate values and performance expectations?

505. Are there trends or hot spots?

506. Sampling part of task?

507. Is this process still needed?

508. What are you trying to accomplish?

509. Are best practices and metrics employed to identify issues, progress, performance, etc.?

510. Who do you send data to?

511. What has the QM Collaboration done?

512. How do senior leaders review organizational performance?

513. How do you decide who is responsible for

signing the data reports?

514. Are there ways to reduce the time it takes to get something approved?

515. Were there any deficiencies / issues identified in the prior years self-assessment?

516. What is quality planning ?

517. Is the amount of effort justified by the anticipated value of forming a new process?

518. Were there any deficiencies / issues in prior years self-assessment?

519. How do you check in-coming sample material?

2.25 Quality Metrics: Data Preparation Tools

520. Are there already quality metrics available that detect nonlinear embeddings and trends similar to the users perception?

521. Is there a set of procedures to capture, analyze and act on quality metrics?

522. Why is now the time for quality metrics?

523. Has it met internal or external standards?

524. Which are the right metrics to use?

525. Are interface issues coordinated?

526. Who notifies stakeholders of normal and abnormal results?

527. How do you measure?

528. Have alternatives been defined in the event that failure occurs?

529. Are applicable standards referenced and available?

530. Were number of defects identified?

531. What is the timeline to meet your goal?

532. How do you calculate such metrics?

533. Did the team meet the Data Preparation Tools project success criteria documented in the Quality Metrics Matrix?

534. Do you stratify metrics by product or site?

535. If the defect rate during testing is substantially higher than that of the previous release (or a similar product), then ask: Did you plan for and actually improve testing effectiveness?

536. Do you know how much profit a 10% decrease in waste would generate?

537. Can visual measures help you to filter visualizations of interest?

538. What group is empowered to define quality requirements?

539. What happens if you get an abnormal result?

2.26 Process Improvement Plan: Data Preparation Tools

540. Does your process ensure quality?

541. Everyone agrees on what process improvement is, right?

542. What is the return on investment?

543. Management commitment at all levels?

544. Has a process guide to collect the data been developed?

545. Why do you want to achieve the goal?

546. Are you making progress on your improvement plan?

547. What personnel are the champions for the initiative?

548. Does explicit definition of the measures exist?

549. Why quality management?

550. Are you following the quality standards?

551. How do you manage quality?

552. To elicit goal statements, do you ask a question such as, What do you want to achieve?

553. Have the frequency of collection and the points in the process where measurements will be made been determined?

554. What is the test-cycle concept?

555. Where do you focus?

556. Where do you want to be?

557. Where are you now?

558. What is quality and how will you ensure it?

2.27 Responsibility Assignment Matrix: Data Preparation Tools

559. Are the wbs and organizational levels for application of the Data Preparation Tools projected overhead costs identified?

560. Identify potential or actual overruns and underruns?

561. Is it safe to say you can handle more work or that some tasks you are supposed to do arent worth doing?

562. How many people do you need?

563. Are data elements reconcilable between internal summary reports and reports forwarded to stakeholders?

564. No rs: if a task has no one listed as responsible, who is getting the job done?

565. What expertise is available in your department?

566. Does the scheduling system identify in a timely manner the status of work?

567. What can you do to improve productivity?

568. Do managers and team members provide helpful suggestions during review meetings?

569. Does the contractor use objective results, design reviews and tests to trace schedule performance?

570. When performing is split among two or more roles, is the work clearly defined so that the efforts are coordinated and the communication is clear?

571. Competencies and craftsmanship – what competencies are necessary and what level?

572. Wbs elements contractually specified for reporting of status (lowest level only)?

573. What is the number one predictor of a groups productivity?

574. Is work progressively subdivided into detailed work packages as requirements are defined?

2.28 Roles and Responsibilities: Data Preparation Tools

575. Required skills, knowledge, experience?

576. Is feedback clearly communicated and non-judgmental?

577. Be specific; avoid generalities. Thank you and great work alone are insufficient. What exactly do you appreciate and why?

578. What specific behaviors did you observe?

579. What expectations were NOT met?

580. How is your work-life balance?

581. Does the team have access to and ability to use data analysis tools?

582. Was the expectation clearly communicated?

583. How well did the Data Preparation Tools project Team understand the expectations of specific roles and responsibilities?

584. Are Data Preparation Tools project team roles and responsibilities identified and documented?

585. What should you highlight for improvement?

586. Where are you most strong as a supervisor?

587. Influence: what areas of organizational decision making are you able to influence when you do not have authority to make the final decision?

588. Who: who is involved?

589. Accountabilities: what are the roles and responsibilities of individual team members?

590. Does your vision/mission support a culture of quality data?

591. Have you ever been a part of this team?

592. To decide whether to use a quality measurement, ask how will you know when it is achieved?

593. What should you do now to ensure that you are meeting all expectations of your current position?

2.29 Human Resource Management Plan: Data Preparation Tools

594. How complete is the human resource management plan?

595. Are people being developed to meet the challenges of the future?

596. Have process improvement efforts been completed before requirements efforts begin?

597. Has a Data Preparation Tools project Communications Plan been developed?

598. Are the payment terms being followed?

599. Are estimating assumptions and constraints captured?

600. Is there a Quality Management Plan?

601. Have external dependencies been captured in the schedule?

602. Does the detailed work plan match the complexity of tasks with the capabilities of personnel?

603. Are multiple estimation methods being employed?

604. How well does your organization communicate?

605. What were things that you did very well and want to do the same again on the next Data Preparation Tools project?

606. Are quality inspections and review activities listed in the Data Preparation Tools project schedule(s)?

607. Are change requests logged and managed?

608. Are vendor invoices audited for accuracy before payment?

609. Data Preparation Tools project Objectives?

610. Are the Data Preparation Tools project plans updated on a frequent basis?

611. How can below standard performers be guided/developed to upgrade performance?

2.30 Communications Management Plan: Data Preparation Tools

612. How much time does it take to do it?

613. Who have you worked with in past, similar initiatives?

614. Who to learn from?

615. What steps can you take for a positive relationship?

616. Do you ask; can you recommend others for you to talk with about this initiative?

617. Are the stakeholders getting the information others need, are others consulted, are concerns addressed?

618. How do you manage communications?

619. Who are the members of the governing body?

620. Will messages be directly related to the release strategy or phases of the Data Preparation Tools project?

621. What is the political influence?

622. Are there common objectives between the team and the stakeholder?

623. Who will use or be affected by the result of a Data Preparation Tools project?

624. Why is stakeholder engagement important?

625. Why do you manage communications?

626. Who is responsible?

627. Which stakeholders can influence others?

628. Where do team members get information?

629. Do you feel a register helps?

630. Who is involved as you identify stakeholders?

631. Why manage stakeholders?

2.31 Risk Management Plan: Data Preparation Tools

632. Is the customer willing to establish rapid communication links with the developer?

633. My Data Preparation Tools project leader has suddenly left your organization, what do you do?

634. Are people attending meetings and doing work?

635. Are Data Preparation Tools project requirements stable?

636. Are the participants able to keep up with the workload?

637. Are certain activities taking a long time to complete?

638. User involvement: do you have the right users?

639. Prioritized components/features?

640. Was an original risk assessment/risk management plan completed?

641. How would you suggest monitoring for risk transition indicators?

642. How risk averse are you?

643. Are the metrics meaningful and useful?

644. How can the process be made more effective or less cumbersome (process improvements)?

645. Why might it be late?

646. Do requirements demand the use of new analysis, design, or testing methods?

647. Does the customer understand the software process?

648. What things are likely to change?

649. Are testing tools available and suitable?

650. What other risks are created by choosing an avoidance strategy?

2.32 Risk Register: Data Preparation Tools

651. What are your key risks/show istoppers and what is being done to manage them?

652. How well are risks controlled?

653. Recovery actions - planned actions taken once a risk has occurred to allow you to move on. What should you do after?

654. What is the reason for current performance gaps and do the risks and opportunities identified previously account for this?

655. When would you develop a risk register?

656. Technology risk -is the Data Preparation Tools project technically feasible?

657. Who needs to know about this?

658. Assume the event happens, what is the Most Likely impact?

659. What are the major risks facing the Data Preparation Tools project?

660. What is your current and future risk profile?

661. Schedule impact/severity estimated range (workdays) assume the event happens, what is the

potential impact?

662. What are the main aims, objectives of the policy, strategy, or service and the intended outcomes?

663. What is a Risk?

664. Who is going to do it?

665. What could prevent you delivering on the strategic program objectives and what is being done to mitigate corresponding issues?

666. Market risk -will the new service or product be useful to your organization or marketable to others?

667. Preventative actions - planned actions to reduce the likelihood a risk will occur and/or reduce the seriousness should it occur. What should you do now?

668. What evidence do you have to justify the likelihood score of the risk (audit, incident report, claim, complaints, inspection, internal review)?

669. How is a Community Risk Register created?

2.33 Probability and Impact Assessment: Data Preparation Tools

670. Will there be an increase in the political conservatism?

671. What is the likelihood?

672. What should be the level of coordination?

673. Is the delay in one subData Preparation Tools project going to affect another?

674. Are the best people available?

675. Can you avoid altogether some things that might go wrong?

676. Your customers business requirements have suddenly shifted because of a new regulatory statute, what now?

677. What can you do to minimize the impact if it does?

678. What is the risk appetite?

679. Are some people working on multiple Data Preparation Tools projects?

680. How do you define a risk?

681. Is the process supported by tools?

682. My Data Preparation Tools project leader has suddenly left your organization, what do you do?

683. Is the number of people on the Data Preparation Tools project team adequate to do the job?

684. Are staff committed for the duration of the Data Preparation Tools project?

685. What are the probabilities of chosen technologies being suitable for local conditions?

686. What risks does your organization have if the Data Preparation Tools projects fail to meet deadline?

687. What is the likelihood of a breakthrough?

688. Is a software Data Preparation Tools project management tool available?

2.34 Probability and Impact Matrix: Data Preparation Tools

689. What are the likely future requirements?

690. What is the best method for analysing the risks for different types of Data Preparation Tools projects?

691. What has the Data Preparation Tools project manager forgotten to do?

692. Are the risk data timely and relevant?

693. What are data sources?

694. Are there new risks that mitigation strategies might introduce?

695. What things might go wrong?

696. Do others match with the clients requirement?

697. What can go wrong?

698. Is security a central objective?

699. What will be the likely political situation during the life of the Data Preparation Tools project?

700. Is the Data Preparation Tools project cutting across the entire organization?

701. Is the number of people on the Data Preparation

Tools project team adequate to do the job?

702. How do you manage Data Preparation Tools project Risk?

703. What are the methods to deal with risks?

704. What are the channels available for distribution to the customer?

705. Do you use any methods to analyze risks?

706. How likely is the current plan to come in on schedule or on budget?

2.35 Risk Data Sheet: Data Preparation Tools

707. Has the most cost-effective solution been chosen?

708. What is the environment within which you operate (social trends, economic, community values, broad based participation, national directions etc.)?

709. Do effective diagnostic tests exist?

710. What will be the consequences if the risk happens?

711. How reliable is the data source?

712. Has a sensitivity analysis been carried out?

713. What is the chance that it will happen?

714. Type of risk identified?

715. Whom do you serve (customers)?

716. What can happen?

717. What if client refuses?

718. What are the main opportunities available to you that you should grab while you can?

719. What is the likelihood of it happening?

720. Is the data sufficiently specified in terms of the type of failure being analyzed, and its frequency or probability?

721. What are you trying to achieve (Objectives)?

722. What actions can be taken to eliminate or remove risk?

723. Risk of what?

724. How do you handle product safely?

725. What was measured?

2.36 Procurement Management Plan: Data Preparation Tools

726. How long will it take for the purchase cost to be the same as the lease cost?

727. Is there a procurement management plan in place?

728. Are all resource assumptions documented?

729. Is the quality assurance team identified?

730. Have all involved Data Preparation Tools project stakeholders and work groups committed to the Data Preparation Tools project?

731. Are software metrics formally captured, analyzed and used as a basis for other Data Preparation Tools project estimates?

732. How will multiple providers be managed?

733. Was your organizations estimating methodology being used and followed?

734. Are the Data Preparation Tools project plans updated on a frequent basis?

735. Has the Data Preparation Tools project manager been identified?

736. Are assumptions being identified, recorded,

analyzed, qualified and closed?

737. Have all necessary approvals been obtained?

738. How will you coordinate Procurement with aspects of the Data Preparation Tools project?

739. Were Data Preparation Tools project team members involved in the development of activity & task decomposition?

2.37 Source Selection Criteria: Data Preparation Tools

740. How will you decide an evaluators write up is sufficient?

741. When must you conduct a debriefing?

742. Does the evaluation of any change include an impact analysis; how will the change affect the scope, time, cost, and quality of the goods or services being provided?

743. Is this a cost contract?

744. What are the limitations on pre-competitive range communications?

745. What documentation is necessary regarding electronic communications?

746. When is it appropriate to issue a DRFP?

747. Do you prepare an independent cost estimate?

748. When should debriefings be held and how should they be scheduled?

749. How are oral presentations documented?

750. What are open book debriefings?

751. Do you have designated specific forms or

worksheets?

752. What is the effect of the debriefing schedule on potential protests?

753. How do you encourage efficiency and consistency?

754. Are there any common areas of weaknesses or deficiencies in the proposals in the competitive range?

755. How will you evaluate offerors proposals?

756. How should the preproposal conference be conducted?

757. What is price analysis and when should it be performed?

758. Are responses to considerations adequate?

759. What is cost analysis and when should it be performed?

2.38 Stakeholder Management Plan: Data Preparation Tools

760. What other teams / processes would be impacted by changes to the current process, and how?

761. Have adequate resources been provided by management to ensure Data Preparation Tools project success?

762. Has a Data Preparation Tools project Communications Plan been developed?

763. Are adequate resources provided for the quality assurance function?

764. Does all Data Preparation Tools project documentation reside in a common repository for easy access?

765. Have all involved stakeholders and work groups committed to the Data Preparation Tools project?

766. When would you develop a Data Preparation Tools project Business Plan?

767. Are internal Data Preparation Tools project status meetings held at reasonable intervals?

768. Are Data Preparation Tools project contact logs kept up to date?

769. Have all unresolved risks been documented?

770. Are risk oriented checklists used during risk identification?

771. What is to be the method of release?

772. Are milestone deliverables effectively tracked and compared to Data Preparation Tools project plan?

773. Are the appropriate IT resources adequate to meet planned commitments?

774. Are formal code reviews conducted?

775. Are there processes in place to ensure internal consistency between the source code components?

776. Does the Data Preparation Tools project have a formal Data Preparation Tools project Charter?

777. Do you use diagrams and tables to account for complex concepts and increase overall readability?

2.39 Change Management Plan: Data Preparation Tools

778. Will the readiness criteria be met prior to the training roll out?

779. What new behaviours are required?

780. Will the culture embrace or reject this change?

781. What are the key change management success metrics?

782. Has the priority for this Data Preparation Tools project been set by the Business Unit Management Team?

783. What new roles are needed?

784. What do you expect the target audience to do, say, think or feel as a result of this communication?

785. How will the stakeholders share information and transfer knowledge?

786. What are the essentials of the message?

787. Have the business unit contacts been briefed by the Data Preparation Tools project team?

788. What new competencies will be required for the roles?

789. What roles within your organization are affected, and how?

790. Has the target training audience been identified and nominated?

791. Where will the funds come from?

792. Change invariability confront many relationships especially the already stated that require a set of behaviours What roles with in your organization are affected and how?

793. What method and medium would you use to announce a message?

794. Who might present the most resistance?

795. What time commitment will this involve?

3.0 Executing Process Group: Data Preparation Tools

796. Just how important is your work to the overall success of the Data Preparation Tools project?

797. Is the program supported by national and/or local organizations?

798. What factors are contributing to progress or delay in the achievement of products and results?

799. Were sponsors and decision makers available when needed outside regularly scheduled meetings?

800. What areas does the group agree are the biggest success on the Data Preparation Tools project?

801. Is activity definition the first process involved in Data Preparation Tools project time management?

802. Why should Data Preparation Tools project managers strive to make jobs look easy?

803. What are deliverables of your Data Preparation Tools project?

804. How will professionals learn what is expected from them what the deliverables are?

805. Who will be the main sponsor?

806. How well defined and documented were

the Data Preparation Tools project management processes you chose to use?

807. What are the main parts of the scope statement?

808. Are the necessary foundations in place to ensure the sustainability of the results of the programme?

809. What were things that you did very well and want to do the same again on the next Data Preparation Tools project?

810. How well did the team follow the chosen processes?

811. Does software appear easy to learn?

812. What good practices or successful experiences or transferable examples have been identified?

813. It under budget or over budget?

3.1 Team Member Status Report: Data Preparation Tools

814. Are your organizations Data Preparation Tools projects more successful over time?

815. Why is it to be done?

816. Does your organization have the means (staff, money, contract, etc.) to produce or to acquire the product, good, or service?

817. When a teams productivity and success depend on collaboration and the efficient flow of information, what generally fails them?

818. How does this product, good, or service meet the needs of the Data Preparation Tools project and your organization as a whole?

819. How will resource planning be done?

820. Is there evidence that staff is taking a more professional approach toward management of your organizations Data Preparation Tools projects?

821. Are the products of your organizations Data Preparation Tools projects meeting customers objectives?

822. Are the attitudes of staff regarding Data Preparation Tools project work improving?

823. How it is to be done?

824. How can you make it practical?

825. What is to be done?

826. Will the staff do training or is that done by a third party?

827. Does every department have to have a Data Preparation Tools project Manager on staff?

828. The problem with Reward & Recognition Programs is that the truly deserving people all too often get left out. How can you make it practical?

829. Does the product, good, or service already exist within your organization?

830. What specific interest groups do you have in place?

831. How much risk is involved?

832. Do you have an Enterprise Data Preparation Tools project Management Office (EPMO)?

3.2 Change Request: Data Preparation Tools

833. Who can suggest changes?

834. How are changes requested (forms, method of communication)?

835. Who is responsible to authorize changes?

836. Is it feasible to use requirements attributes as predictors of reliability?

837. How fast will change requests be approved?

838. Will this change conflict with other requirements changes (e.g., lead to conflicting operational scenarios)?

839. What type of changes does change control take into account?

840. Will all change requests be unconditionally tracked through this process?

841. Can static requirements change attributes like the size of the change be used to predict reliability in execution?

842. How many lines of code must be changed to implement the change?

843. Are there requirements attributes that can

discriminate between high and low reliability?

844. How are the measures for carrying out the change established?

845. Who is responsible for the implementation and monitoring of all measures?

846. What can be filed?

847. What kind of information about the change request needs to be captured?

848. How do you get changes (code) out in a timely manner?

849. What is the function of the change control committee?

850. Have scm procedures for noting the change, recording it, and reporting it been followed?

851. Why do you want to have a change control system?

3.3 Change Log: Data Preparation Tools

852. Where do changes come from?

853. When was the request approved?

854. Does the suggested change request represent a desired enhancement to the products functionality?

855. Is this a mandatory replacement?

856. Is the change backward compatible without limitations?

857. Who initiated the change request?

858. When was the request submitted?

859. Is the change request within Data Preparation Tools project scope?

860. Is the change request open, closed or pending?

861. How does this change affect the timeline of the schedule?

862. Is the submitted change a new change or a modification of a previously approved change?

863. Should a more thorough impact analysis be conducted?

864. How does this change affect scope?

865. Is the requested change request a result of changes in other Data Preparation Tools project(s)?

866. Do the described changes impact on the integrity or security of the system?

867. How does this relate to the standards developed for specific business processes?

868. Will the Data Preparation Tools project fail if the change request is not executed?

3.4 Decision Log: Data Preparation Tools

869. What makes you different or better than others companies selling the same thing?

870. With whom was the decision shared or considered?

871. Who will be given a copy of this document and where will it be kept?

872. How does provision of information, both in terms of content and presentation, influence acceptance of alternative strategies?

873. Behaviors; what are guidelines that the team has identified that will assist them with getting the most out of team meetings?

874. At what point in time does loss become unacceptable?

875. Is everything working as expected?

876. Does anything need to be adjusted?

877. What was the rationale for the decision?

878. How effective is maintaining the log at facilitating organizational learning?

879. What is the line where eDiscovery ends and

document review begins?

880. How do you define success?

881. What is the average size of your matters in an applicable measurement?

882. Who is the decisionmaker?

883. Decision-making process; how will the team make decisions?

884. What alternatives/risks were considered?

885. What is your overall strategy for quality control / quality assurance procedures?

886. Do strategies and tactics aimed at less than full control reduce the costs of management or simply shift the cost burden?

887. What eDiscovery problem or issue did your organization set out to fix or make better?

888. How does an increasing emphasis on cost containment influence the strategies and tactics used?

3.5 Quality Audit: Data Preparation Tools

889. How does your organization know that its staff have appropriate access to a fair and effective grievance process?

890. Are all records associated with the reconditioning of a device maintained for a minimum of two years after the sale or disposal of the last device within a lot of merchandise?

891. How does your organization know that its Mission, Vision and Values Statements are appropriate and effectively guiding your organization?

892. What does an analysis of your organizations staff profile suggest in terms of its planning, and how is this being addressed?

893. How does your organization know whether they are adhering to mission and achieving objectives?

894. How does your organization know that its relationships with the community at large are appropriately effective and constructive?

895. Health and safety arrangements; stress management workshops. How does your organization know that it provides a safe and healthy environment?

896. Are multiple statements on the same issue consistent with each other?

897. Are all staff empowered and encouraged to contribute to ongoing improvement efforts?

898. Are the policies and processes, as set out in the Quality Audit Manual, properly applied?

899. How does your organization know that its research programs are appropriately effective and constructive?

900. Are complaint files maintained?

901. Are the review comments incorporated?

902. How does your organization know that its system for recruiting the best staff possible are appropriately effective and constructive?

903. How does your organization know that its Governance system is appropriately effective and constructive?

904. Are all employees made aware of device defects which may occur from the improper performance of specific jobs?

905. Is your organizational structure a help or a hindrance to deployment?

906. How does your organization know that its planning processes are appropriately effective and constructive?

907. Are adequate and conveniently located toilet facilities available for use by the employees?

908. How does the organization know that its industry and community engagement planning and management systems are appropriately effective and constructive in enabling relationships with key stakeholder groups?

3.6 Team Directory: Data Preparation Tools

909. Where should the information be distributed?

910. How do unidentified risks impact the outcome of the Data Preparation Tools project?

911. Days from the time the issue is identified?

912. Who are your stakeholders (customers, sponsors, end users, team members)?

913. Process decisions: are there any statutory or regulatory issues relevant to the timely execution of work?

914. Who are the Team Members?

915. Process decisions: which organizational elements and which individuals will be assigned management functions?

916. Do purchase specifications and configurations match requirements?

917. Who is the Sponsor?

918. How will the team handle changes?

919. When does information need to be distributed?

920. Have you decided when to celebrate the Data

Preparation Tools projects completion date?

921. Where will the product be used and/or delivered or built when appropriate?

922. Who will talk to the customer?

923. How and in what format should information be presented?

924. How will you accomplish and manage the objectives?

925. Timing: when do the effects of communication take place?

926. Process decisions: how well was task order work performed?

927. How does the team resolve conflicts and ensure tasks are completed?

3.7 Team Operating Agreement: Data Preparation Tools

928. What went well?

929. Have you set the goals and objectives of the team?

930. What are the current caseload numbers in the unit?

931. What individual strengths does each team member bring to the group?

932. Do team members need to frequently communicate as a full group to make timely decisions?

933. What are the safety issues/risks that need to be addressed and/or that the team needs to consider?

934. Do you vary your voice pace, tone and pitch to engage participants and gain involvement?

935. Must your members collaborate successfully to complete Data Preparation Tools projects?

936. Are there the right people on your team?

937. Are there more than two native languages represented by your team?

938. To whom do you deliver your services?

939. Did you prepare participants for the next meeting?

940. Do you prevent individuals from dominating the meeting?

941. Are there differences in access to communication and collaboration technology based on team member location?

942. Conflict resolution: how will disputes and other conflicts be mediated or resolved?

943. What is the number of cases currently teamed?

944. Do you post meeting notes and the recording (if used) and notify participants?

945. Do you send out the agenda and meeting materials in advance?

946. Do you begin with a question to engage everyone?

3.8 Team Performance Assessment: Data Preparation Tools

947. Can familiarity breed backup?

948. To what degree are the teams goals and objectives clear, simple, and measurable?

949. What are teams?

950. To what degree does the teams approach to its work allow for modification and improvement over time?

951. To what degree does the teams purpose constitute a broader, deeper aspiration than just accomplishing short-term goals?

952. What do you think is the most constructive thing that could be done now to resolve considerations and disputes about method variance?

953. To what degree do team members frequently explore the teams purpose and its implications?

954. How hard did you try to make a good selection?

955. Delaying market entry: how long is too long?

956. To what degree can all members engage in open and interactive considerations?

957. What structural changes have you made or are

you preparing to make?

958. To what degree are fresh input and perspectives systematically caught and added (for example, through information and analysis, new members, and senior sponsors)?

959. To what degree do team members agree with the goals, relative importance, and the ways in which achievement will be measured?

960. To what degree does the teams purpose contain themes that are particularly meaningful and memorable?

961. To what degree are the relative importance and priority of the goals clear to all team members?

962. Which situations call for a more extreme type of adaptiveness in which team members actually re-define roles?

963. How hard do you try to make a good selection?

964. To what degree will the approach capitalize on and enhance the skills of all team members in a manner that takes into consideration other demands on members of the team?

965. To what degree will new and supplemental skills be introduced as the need is recognized?

966. To what degree can the team ensure that all members are individually and jointly accountable for the teams purpose, goals, approach, and work-products?

3.9 Team Member Performance Assessment: Data Preparation Tools

967. What are the standards or expectations for success?

968. How are performance measures and associated incentives developed?

969. To what degree does the team possess adequate membership to achieve its ends?

970. What are top priorities?

971. Do the goals support your organizations goals?

972. What are the key duties or tasks of the Ratee?

973. Are the draft goals SMART ?

974. What are the basic principles and objectives of performance measurement and assessment?

975. What were the challenges that resulted for training and assessment?

976. To what degree is the team cognizant of small wins to be celebrated along the way?

977. How are assessments designed, delivered, and otherwise used to maximize training?

978. How do you use data to inform instruction and

improve staff achievement?

979. How accurately is your plan implemented?

980. To what degree can the team measure progress against specific goals?

981. Does platform-specific assessment information contribute to training placement or tailoring of instruction (e.g. aptitude-treatment interaction)?

982. What happens if a team member disagrees with the Job Expectations?

983. Does the rater (supervisor) have to wait for the interim or final performance assessment review to tell an employee that the employees performance is unsatisfactory?

984. New skills/knowledge gained this year?

3.10 Issue Log: Data Preparation Tools

985. What steps can you take for positive relationships?

986. Who reported the issue?

987. Are they needed?

988. What is a change?

989. What effort will a change need?

990. Who were proponents/opponents?

991. Is the issue log kept in a safe place?

992. Who is the stakeholder?

993. How often do you engage with stakeholders?

994. Who do you turn to if you have questions?

995. Are there too many who have an interest in some aspect of your work?

996. What is the stakeholders level of authority?

997. Do you have members of your team responsible for certain stakeholders?

998. Are you constantly rushing from meeting to meeting?

999. In your work, how much time is spent on stakeholder identification?

1000. How do you reply to this question; you am new here and managing this major program. How do you suggest you build your network?

4.0 Monitoring and Controlling Process Group: Data Preparation Tools

1001. Do the products created live up to the necessary quality?

1002. How do you monitor progress?

1003. Where is the Risk in the Data Preparation Tools project?

1004. Is progress on outcomes due to your program?

1005. What resources are necessary?

1006. Based on your Data Preparation Tools project communication management plan, what worked well?

1007. Contingency planning. if a risk event occurs, what will you do?

1008. Is it what was agreed upon?

1009. Did it work?

1010. Are the services being delivered?

1011. How are you doing?

1012. User: who wants the information and what are they interested in?

1013. Did you implement the program as designed?

1014. Who are the Data Preparation Tools project stakeholders?

1015. What were things that you did very well and want to do the same again on the next Data Preparation Tools project?

1016. What will you do to minimize the impact should a risk event occur?

1017. Is the verbiage used appropriate and understandable?

1018. Is there sufficient funding available for this?

4.1 Project Performance Report: Data Preparation Tools

1019. To what degree does the information network communicate information relevant to the task?

1020. To what degree does the information network provide individuals with the information they require?

1021. To what degree are the goals realistic?

1022. To what degree does the task meet individual needs?

1023. To what degree can team members vigorously define the teams purpose in considerations with others who are not part of the functioning team?

1024. To what degree do the goals specify concrete team work products?

1025. To what degree does the formal organization make use of individual resources and meet individual needs?

1026. To what degree are the skill areas critical to team performance present?

1027. How can Data Preparation Tools project sustainability be maintained?

1028. To what degree is the information network consistent with the structure of the formal organization?

1029. To what degree does the teams work approach provide opportunity for members to engage in results-based evaluation?

1030. To what degree do team members feel that the purpose of the team is important, if not exciting?

1031. What is in it for you?

1032. To what degree is there centralized control of information sharing?

1033. How is the data used?

1034. To what degree do the structures of the formal organization motivate taskrelevant behavior and facilitate task completion?

1035. To what degree does the informal organization make use of individual resources and meet individual needs?

4.2 Variance Analysis: Data Preparation Tools

1036. Does the accounting system provide a basis for auditing records of direct costs chargeable to the contract?

1037. Are the bases and rates for allocating costs from each indirect pool consistently applied?

1038. Is cost and schedule performance measurement done in a consistent, systematic manner?

1039. What is the dollar amount of the fluctuation?

1040. What is the budgeted cost for work scheduled?

1041. What costs are avoidable if one or more customers are dropped?

1042. How do you identify and isolate causes of favorable and unfavorable cost and schedule variances?

1043. Is the market likely to continue to grow at this rate next year?

1044. Are overhead costs budgets established on a basis consistent with the anticipated direct business base?

1045. Do you identify potential or actual budget-based and time-based schedule variances?

1046. What is the incurrence of actual indirect costs in excess of budgets, by element of expense?

1047. Why are standard cost systems used?

1048. Favorable or unfavorable variance?

1049. Are management actions taken to reduce indirect costs when there are significant adverse variances?

1050. How have the setting and use of standards changed over time?

1051. How do you evaluate the impact of schedule changes, work around, et?

1052. Can the contractor substantiate work package and planning package budgets?

1053. What is your organizations rationale for sharing expenses and services between business segments?

4.3 Earned Value Status: Data Preparation Tools

1054. Where is evidence-based earned value in your organization reported?

1055. Earned value can be used in almost any Data Preparation Tools project situation and in almost any Data Preparation Tools project environment. it may be used on large Data Preparation Tools projects, medium sized Data Preparation Tools projects, tiny Data Preparation Tools projects (in cut-down form), complex and simple Data Preparation Tools projects and in any market sector. some people, of course, know all about earned value, they have used it for years - but perhaps not as effectively as they could have?

1056. Are you hitting your Data Preparation Tools projects targets?

1057. Where are your problem areas?

1058. What is the unit of forecast value?

1059. Validation is a process of ensuring that the developed system will actually achieve the stakeholders desired outcomes; Are you building the right product? What do you validate?

1060. When is it going to finish?

1061. Verification is a process of ensuring that

the developed system satisfies the stakeholders agreements and specifications; Are you building the product right? What do you verify?

1062. How much is it going to cost by the finish?

1063. How does this compare with other Data Preparation Tools projects?

1064. If earned value management (EVM) is so good in determining the true status of a Data Preparation Tools project and Data Preparation Tools project its completion, why is it that hardly any one uses it in information systems related Data Preparation Tools projects?

4.4 Risk Audit: Data Preparation Tools

1065. Mitigation -how can you avoid the risk?

1066. How are risk appetites expressed?

1067. Are requirements fully understood by the team and customers?

1068. Do you have written and signed agreements/ contracts in place for each paid staff member?

1069. Improving fraud detection: do auditors react to abnormal inconsistencies between financial and non-financial measures?

1070. Will safety checks of personal equipment supplied by competitors be conducted?

1071. Auditor independence: a burdensome constraint or a core value?

1072. Are auditors able to effectively apply more soft evidence found in the risk-assessment process with the results of more tangible audit evidence found through more substantive testing?

1073. Assessing risk with analytical procedures: do systemsthinking tools help auditors focus on diagnostic patterns?

1074. Do you have a realistic budget and do you present regular financial reports that identify how you are going against that budget?

1075. What is the anticipated volatility of the requirements?

1076. Are risk management strategies documented?

1077. Do you have financial policies and procedures in place to guide officers of your organization/treasurer/general members?

1078. What events or circumstances could affect the achievement of your objectives?

1079. Management -what contingency plans do you have if the risk becomes a reality?

1080. Number of users of the product?

1081. What are the benefits of a Enterprise wide approach to Risk Management?

1082. Is the auditor able to evaluate contradictory evidence in an unbiased manner?

1083. To what extent are auditors effective at linking business risks and management assertions?

1084. Does your organization have a social media policy and procedure?

4.5 Contractor Status Report: Data Preparation Tools

1085. How long have you been using the services?

1086. What was the overall budget or estimated cost?

1087. What was the actual budget or estimated cost for your organizations services?

1088. How is risk transferred?

1089. Who can list a Data Preparation Tools project as organization experience, your organization or a previous employee of your organization?

1090. If applicable; describe your standard schedule for new software version releases. Are new software version releases included in the standard maintenance plan?

1091. Describe how often regular updates are made to the proposed solution. Are corresponding regular updates included in the standard maintenance plan?

1092. What process manages the contracts?

1093. Are there contractual transfer concerns?

1094. What are the minimum and optimal bandwidth requirements for the proposed solution?

1095. What is the average response time for

answering a support call?

1096. What was the budget or estimated cost for your organizations services?

1097. What was the final actual cost?

4.6 Formal Acceptance: Data Preparation Tools

1098. What function(s) does it fill or meet?

1099. Was the Data Preparation Tools project goal achieved?

1100. Was the Data Preparation Tools project managed well?

1101. Was the Data Preparation Tools project work done on time, within budget, and according to specification?

1102. Was the client satisfied with the Data Preparation Tools project results?

1103. What was done right?

1104. Was the sponsor/customer satisfied?

1105. Who would use it?

1106. Did the Data Preparation Tools project manager and team act in a professional and ethical manner?

1107. Was business value realized?

1108. How does your team plan to obtain formal acceptance on your Data Preparation Tools project?

1109. Does it do what client said it would?

1110. What is the Acceptance Management Process?

1111. Do you buy-in installation services?

1112. What are the requirements against which to test, Who will execute?

1113. Do you buy pre-configured systems or build your own configuration?

1114. Is formal acceptance of the Data Preparation Tools project product documented and distributed?

1115. Who supplies data?

1116. General estimate of the costs and times to complete the Data Preparation Tools project?

1117. Do you perform formal acceptance or burn-in tests?

5.0 Closing Process Group: Data Preparation Tools

1118. Are there funding or time constraints?

1119. What level of risk does the proposed budget represent to the Data Preparation Tools project?

1120. What can you do better next time, and what specific actions can you take to improve?

1121. What areas were overlooked on this Data Preparation Tools project?

1122. Who are the Data Preparation Tools project stakeholders?

1123. Does the close educate others to improve performance?

1124. Is the Data Preparation Tools project funded?

1125. What areas does the group agree are the biggest success on the Data Preparation Tools project?

1126. What was learned?

1127. Did you do things well?

1128. How will you do it?

1129. Was the schedule met?

1130. What is the Data Preparation Tools project Management Process?

1131. How dependent is the Data Preparation Tools project on other Data Preparation Tools projects or work efforts?

5.1 Procurement Audit: Data Preparation Tools

1132. Have guidelines been set up for how the procurement process should be conducted?

1133. Are information gathered to produce knowledge about procured goods and services, prices paid and supplier performance?

1134. In the set up of the system and in the award of contracts were only electronic means used?

1135. Was the expert likely to gain privileged knowledge from his activity which could be advantageous for him in a subsequent competition?

1136. Are all initial purchase contracts made by the purchasing organization?

1137. Has it been determined which areas of procurement the audit should cover?

1138. Was the award criterion only the most economical advantageous tender?

1139. Do at least two people have custodial responsibilities for negotiable checks (one checking on the other)?

1140. Was the award decision based on the result of the evaluation of tenders?

1141. Does the strategy ensure that appropriate controls are in place to ensure propriety and regularity in delivery?

1142. Were bids properly evaluated?

1143. Are there procedures for trade-in arrangements?

1144. Did the conditions of contract comply with the detail provided in the procurement documents and with the outcome of the procurement procedure followed?

1145. Did your organization decide upon an adequate and admissible procurement procedure?

1146. Are approval limits covered in written procedures?

1147. Have guidelines incorporating the principles and objectives of a robust procurement practice been established?

1148. Are risks in the external environment identified, for example: Budgetary constraints?

1149. Is a log maintained over the use of signature plates?

1150. Are all complaints of late or incorrect payment sent to a person independent of the already stated having cash disbursement responsibilities?

1151. Has your organization examined in detail the definition of performance?

5.2 Contract Close-Out: Data Preparation Tools

1152. What is capture management?

1153. Have all contract records been included in the Data Preparation Tools project archives?

1154. Change in attitude or behavior?

1155. Have all contracts been completed?

1156. Change in circumstances?

1157. Was the contract complete without requiring numerous changes and revisions?

1158. Was the contract type appropriate?

1159. What happens to the recipient of services?

1160. Why Outsource?

1161. Parties: Authorized?

1162. Change in knowledge?

1163. Has each contract been audited to verify acceptance and delivery?

1164. How is the contracting office notified of the automatic contract close-out?

1165. Have all contracts been closed?

1166. Parties: who is involved?

1167. How does it work?

1168. Are the signers the authorized officials?

1169. Was the contract sufficiently clear so as not to result in numerous disputes and misunderstandings?

1170. Have all acceptance criteria been met prior to final payment to contractors?

1171. How/when used ?

5.3 Project or Phase Close-Out: Data Preparation Tools

1172. Were messages directly related to the release strategy or phases of the Data Preparation Tools project?

1173. Does the lesson educate others to improve performance?

1174. What benefits or impacts does the stakeholder group expect to obtain as a result of the Data Preparation Tools project?

1175. Can the lesson learned be replicated?

1176. What is a Risk Management Process?

1177. Were cost budgets met?

1178. What are the mandatory communication needs for each stakeholder?

1179. What is the information level of detail required for each stakeholder?

1180. Planned completion date?

1181. What was the preferred delivery mechanism?

1182. What could be done to improve the process?

1183. Which changes might a stakeholder be required

to make as a result of the Data Preparation Tools project?

1184. Were risks identified and mitigated?

1185. How often did each stakeholder need an update?

1186. Did the Data Preparation Tools project management methodology work?

1187. Does the lesson describe a function that would be done differently the next time?

1188. Have business partners been involved extensively, and what data was required for them?

1189. What was expected from each stakeholder?

5.4 Lessons Learned: Data Preparation Tools

1190. What is the frequency of communication?

1191. Who is responsible for each action?

1192. How closely did deliverables match what was defined within the Data Preparation Tools project Scope?

1193. What are the influence patterns?

1194. What are the Benefits of Measurements?

1195. How comprehensive was integration testing?

1196. Where do you go from here?

1197. What did you put in place to ensure success?

1198. What things mattered the most on this Data Preparation Tools project?

1199. What is the frequency of personal communications?

1200. What needs to be done over or differently?

1201. How clearly defined were the objectives for this Data Preparation Tools project?

1202. Was sufficient time allocated to review Data

Preparation Tools project deliverables?

1203. How extensive is middle management?

1204. How effective was each Data Preparation Tools project Team member in fulfilling his/her role?

1205. How effective was Data Preparation Tools project Team member training?

1206. Did the Data Preparation Tools project improve the team members reputations, skills, personal development?

1207. How effective were Best Practices & Lessons Learned from prior Data Preparation Tools projects utilized in this Data Preparation Tools project?

1208. What is the expected lifespan of the deliverable?

Index

283

CPSIA information can be obtained
at www.ICGtesting.com
Printed in the USA
BVHW041010200819
556236BV00011B/688/P